MW01118747

He Said I Could

Extraordinary From the Ordinary

Robert Streusel

iUniverse, Inc.
New York Bloomington

He Said I Could
Extraordinary From the Ordinary

iUniverse books may be ordered through booksellers or by contacting:

iUniverse
1663 Liberty Drive
Bloomington, IN 47403
www.iuniverse.com
1-800-Authors (1-800-288-4677)

ISBN: 978-1-4502-6678-9 (pbk)
ISBN: 978-1-4502-6679-6 (cloth)
ISBN: 978-1-4502-6680-2 (ebk)

Printed in the United States of America

iUniverse rev. date: 11/10/10

Acknowledgements

First and foremost, I thank God Almighty and my Lord Jesus for showing unfathomable love and mercy to me. No living thing deserves the love that God showers on me daily, or the sacrifice that Jesus provided for me.

I owe much gratitude to my parents for their sacrifices and love. I thank my son and daughter for their help and encouragement. For my good friend Mary who gave me lots of encouragement, I'm very grateful.

And last but certainly not least, I give thanks and praise to God for the wife that He has given me. What a blessing she has been! No man deserves more, and none could expect better. To God be the glory… now and forever more!

Table of Contents

Prologue

With Donald facing me, I bound the spirit of osteoporosis and commanded that spirit to come out of him. Then I bound the spirit of pain and commanded that spirit to come out of him. I commanded the bone mass to stop decreasing and to increase and return to normal. Each time something was commanded or a spirit bound, it was done in the name of Jesus. Donald began to sway slightly and headed for a nearby chair. He said his knees and legs suddenly got weak. I told him that was the Holy Spirit working on him! After a few minutes of sitting, Donald stood up STRAIGHT and WITHOUT PAIN, and left my office (still somewhat wobbly). James 5:17–18 states; *"Elijah was a man just like us. He prayed earnestly that it would not rain, and it did not rain on the land for three and a half years. Again he prayed, and the heavens gave rain, and the earth produced its crops."* We don't normally think about this marvelous statement, assuming that all the prophets of the Bible must have been really special people. The truth is that they were only special because God chose them! We have evidence that they had wives (Hosea 1:3, 2 Kings 4:1), children (Isaiah 7:3), and tempers (Jonah 4:1, 2 Kings 2:23–24). They bought land (Jeremiah 32:9), lived in houses (2 Kings 5:9), and even were afraid (1 Kings 19:3). Sounds pretty much like us.

I know I've heard the Scripture about Elijah being "a man just like us" many times, but once it really hit me, I understood very clearly that *God can use anyone*! Even though I consider myself very average, God has allowed me to be the recipient of miracles, as well as the dispenser of miracles for others.

As you read this book, I want you to be encouraged and believe that God can do more (even through you) than your mind can comprehend. You will read about my own healing and about Donald and Janet who were both healed from Osteoporosis. The stories even contain the healing of people who were not present at the time, just like the story in Matthew 8:5–13 about the Centurion's slave. Be encouraged. Increase your faith. Also know from this book, that I am an ordinary person with no special qualifications or gifts, except for the gift of the Holy Spirit, Who is available to *everyone*!

The names in the book have been changed to protect the privacy of those involved, but all stories are true and not embellished in any way.

The message is simply this: God can, and wants to use you, too. I pray He does! "He said I could" means just that. Jesus said we could use his name to see miracles. (Mark 9:38–40, Mark 16:17, Luke 9:49–50, Luke 10:17, John 14:13–14, John 15:16, John 16:23, John 16:26–27, Acts 3:6–8, Acts 3:16, Acts 4:10)

BOOK 1 – The Funny Side of Life

Chapter I: An Ordinary Son

Ground Cellar Imprisonment

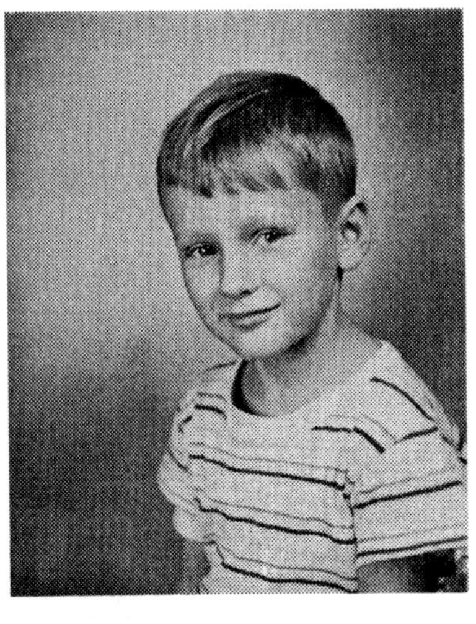

Despite red hair that might indicate otherwise, my mother was always a very gentle, patient woman. She worked very hard taking care of my brother and I, and often other relatives as well. Nursing homes were unheard of in the 40's and 50's, at least in small towns. Mom's elderly mother and Aunt lived in the next small town, only about a mile and a half away, so she made the daily drive to clean, prepare lunch and pick up the washing. That often left me in the house alone which was not always a good thing. Usually, Mom made lunch for us before leaving and left me to clean up the dishes. I could spend an hour playing in the suds, but then I would usually find some mischief to occupy my mind and hands.

In summer and fall, we all busily picked vegetables and fruits to can or freeze, Mom always maintained her mild and patient demeanor, at least until I discovered the limit to her patience.

Mom would be the first to tell you that as a youngster, I tested everyone's patience. One particular day— I don't remember what

I had done—my mother finally reached her limit and didn't know what to do with me. (Murder was pretty rare back then.)

Behind our house maybe 150 feet or so, was Dad's woodworking shop and beneath the shop was an earth cellar. Access to the cellar was only available through a trap door in the floor of the shop.

Whatever I had done had an immediate reaction. Mom picked me up and threw me over her shoulder like a sack of potatoes, and carried me from inside the house to Dad's workshop. Once there, Mom lifted the trap door to the cellar, climbed down the rough open wooden stairs and put me down. She then climbed back up the stairs, closed the trap door and stood on it. The cellar was dark, damp, cool, and spider webs were everywhere. I screamed and begged, but only after I promised to behave, did she release me from my prison. I think I was pretty good for a while after that. In fact, that may have been a small turning point in my life. I like to think that I never misbehaved that badly since then, but it could be that Mom just couldn't throw me over her shoulder anymore.

"He who spares his rod hates his son, but he who loves him disciplines him promptly." (Proverbs 13:24)

Running Naked

When my neighbor Brent and I were very young, we found some old clothes, hats, and shoes in my attic and decided to play "dress–up." We brought the items downstairs and tried them on, first stripping down to our underwear. We soon began challenging each other to run naked to Dad's woodworking shop. A row of pine trees grew across the yard midway between the house and woodshop, but they did not block the view from either of our neighbor's houses. To one side, the neighbor's house was very close—just the width of a driveway—but on the other side between my house and Brent's house, there was an empty lot that we farmed.

Brent and I peered out of the back door and, not seeing anyone in either direction, we took off running. When we got to the pine trees, we stopped to again check for neighbors. That's when we heard Brent's mother yell, "I see you, but I'll look the other way while you run back to the house." She had been blocked from our view by our garage but now stood in plain sight, hanging clothes on the wash line in Brent's back yard. Brent and I quickly ran back to the house, embarrassed, our brief streaking career reaching an abrupt end. Ideas always sound better if you don't consider the possible outcome.

Darts

My brother Greg and I were throwing darts at a cardboard box in our basement when he somehow convinced me to get into the box. He threw a few darts while I complained loudly about being in the box. Just as I stuck my head up to face him and say I was getting out of the box, he threw another dart. The dart somehow stuck firmly in the back of my neck even though I was facing him. My screams of pain and surprise got my dad's attention. He came downstairs, two steps at a time, pulled the dart out of my neck and then threw the darts against the cement wall until they were unusable, which caused me to scream even louder. I was more upset over Dad ruining the darts than I was about having a dart stuck in my neck. Dad then drove me to the doctor's office in the next town. The doctor said I was very fortunate and if the dart had been one–quarter inch away in any direction, I could have been paralyzed. Greg and I were both a lot older before we could play with real darts again.

Run–away

Why I survived childhood, God only knows. It isn't that I lived such a dangerous life, but I had a short temper and was quite rebellious. Mom used to tell me that she was going to give me to the "rag man" someday. The rag man came around door–to–door now and then, collecting rags and selling rags, and he didn't look like the type of person who would have any patience with whiney little boys! I doubted she would do it, but I wasn't absolutely sure.

One day the tables were turned. I was mad at Mom for some reason. I told her I was going to run away. To my surprise she said, "Okay." I didn't know anything about running away nor did I know where to go. There really wasn't anyplace I wanted to go. But my bluff being called, I rode off on my bike—All the way across the street to the town water tower. The water tower was surrounded by large pine trees, and was situated next to an over–grown nursery. It was the perfect place to hide out for a while. I sat down under one of the large pine trees and waited and waited. Finally, realizing it must be close to lunch time I got on my bike and rode back across the street to our house. I walked in expecting my mom to be happy to see me again, but she made no obvious notice that I had even been gone. I was so deflated because I hadn't upset her (at least as far as I knew), that I never threatened to run away again.

Canada Rowboat

Dad took our family to Canada twice when I was young. On one trip we stayed at a lodge in a national park in Quebec. The lodge was built on the shore of a large lake, and had a small square dock, with a small humped bridge over the opening to the lake. My brother Greg and I enjoyed taking turns rowing a small boat inside the protected area created by the docks. We also fished with a bare hook on a piece of string. Dropping it into the water, we caught sun fish after sun fish. No bait required. The sun fish would bite on anything. The only bad part was the mosquitoes. They were biting as well, especially my nearly shaved head, which was called a "teddy bear" haircut. I ended up with more itching bumps on my head than I could count!

One day, as Greg and I were playing with the row boat, we began a brotherly argument about the length of time each of us spent in the boat. After finally convincing Greg that it was my turn, I got into the boat—unfortunately leaving one oar behind on the dock. Greg put that oar to good use, splashing me by hitting the oar on the water. The wetter I got, the angrier I got until I finally retaliated by taking one big swing with my oar. The oar barely skimmed the water causing me to lose my balance and fall head–over–heels into the water. Of course that ended my fun in the rowboat for a while. (Never seek revenge when you're angry, but wait to get even when you can think coolly.) *"Do not seek revenge or bear a grudge against one of your people, but love your neighbor as yourself. I am the LORD."* (Leviticus 19:18)

Lima Beans and Peas

I like lima beans now, but when I was young I hated them. My parents thought that the bigger the bean, the better it was. They let the beans grow on the stalk until the pods were ready to burst. Mom cooked the large lima beans until they were well–done. One lima bean could instantly suck all the moisture out of my mouth, requiring a glass of water with each bean just to get it to go down! (Ok, maybe just a little exaggeration.)

I hated picking lima beans even more than eating them. Mom took me with her to the field and we started at the same end of adjacent rows. I gingerly lifted each leaf to see if there was a yellow fuzzy bug underneath because a yellow bug "smooshed" on my hand left a yellow stain. My progress was extremely slow. I had a metal bucket to put the beans into, but I sat on it. Eventually, I put a few beans into the bucket but Mom finished her row and started back toward me in a new row before I was a third of the way down my row. Dad spanked me and threatened to "beat my rear end" even more, but I still sat on the bucket and didn't pick many beans.

Peas were a different story. I never disliked eating peas; I just didn't like to shell them. My thumb got sore from opening the pods and the underside of my thumbnail remained green for a week. The benefit to all the work was a year–round supply of homegrown (Fresh and frozen) peas to eat.

Every year we had a problem with black birds in the pea patch. They were very sneaky, landing at the end of a row far from the house, then walking up the row, peeking over the plants once in a while to see if the coast was clear. We tied tin pie plates on strings hung from poles, made scare crows and tried other remedies, but the birds just ignored our efforts. Then we went from defense to offense.

Dad got some cherry bombs and we found a way to detonate them remotely. After making a small hole through the base of the fuse with a pin, a piece of very thin copper wire was inserted through the hole and tied to the end of a long extension cord. We placed the cherry bomb between two rows in the middle of the field and ran the extension cord back to the garage. From inside the garage we watched the field—ready to plug in the cord and detonate the cherry bomb any time a black bird got close to it. This kept the birds away for longer periods of time so we didn't have to repeat it too often.

One time a black bird landed very near the cherry bomb so we plugged in the extension cord, and the bird flew into the air, tail over beak. The bird must have assumed the cherry bomb was a real cherry, and went for it. That was one black bird that didn't live to eat another day.

For a while we tried shooting the birds with a .22 caliber rifle. One day a policeman showed up at our house and asked if we had been shooting a rifle. We admitted to shooting at birds in our field. He then he told us that a neighbor (behind our property) had a bullet hole in the front door of his house. The policeman asked us to be more careful and left. After that we only used a pellet gun.

Chalk it on Ice

In late summer, my parents would send me down the main street of our town, to sell produce from our garden. My red wagon was loaded with green beans, lima beans, squash and other vegetables. I didn't like selling. I was never good about adding up the cost and figuring out the change. One day after selling a few things along the way, I arrived at my grandmother's house several doors down the street. She selected some vegetables and when I told her how much they were, she said, "Chalk it on ice." Having never heard that expression before, I asked what she meant. She said she didn't need to pay. I was very disappointed. When I got home and told Dad, he was angry, but Mom said, "Never mind about it."

Rapture?

Freddie and I became friends in church as youngsters, and together we sang in the choir. There were three churches in our town; the Lutheran Church, the Evangelical Church and the United Brethren Church. The evangelical and United Brethren churches combined, becoming the Evangelical United Brethren Church, and since the two buildings were around the corner from each other, one building was used for the church services and the other was used for the youth building and some of the Sunday school classes. Both buildings were small white frame buildings with a steeple, like any small town church across America. This is the church that I grew up in.

The choir loft was located behind the pulpit, and a Gothic arch created an opening between the choir and congregation, allowing the choir to be seen by the congregation. One Sunday morning as I looked around the sanctuary, I noticed a few cracks in the ceiling. I whispered to Freddie about the cracks, and he looked with me. As we checked out the spider web–like cracks on the ceiling, I suddenly realized that the congregation could see us. I looked out across the congregation to see everyone in the pews also looking at the ceiling! The preacher, who couldn't see us behind him, had to wonder why everyone in the congregation was staring at the ceiling. I'm sure he must have felt rather anxious, maybe even thinking the rapture had begun and everyone knew it but him!

During one Christmas season, as we sang the Christmas cantata, Freddie and I were in the back row of the choir, on the next to the top step of the altar area. The steps were wooden, and any shifting of weight or movement of any kind created a creaking noise. The old wood, though carpeted, also seemed to amplify footsteps, so we tried moving as little as possible.

Choir robes are normally quite warm, but with the addition of a full sanctuary and the heating system going full blast, a sauna more aptly describes how it felt.

As a youngster, I suffered from extremely high blood pressure—in fact, our family doctor once said he had never seen blood pressure as high as mine in a young person. High blood pressure, coupled with the heat, caused me to pass out near the end of the cantata. Because the choir members stood shoulder to shoulder, there was nowhere to go but down, so I sat on the top step with a "THUMP." Our Choir Director heard the thump and (as he told me later) immediately thought, "I wonder what those boys are up to now!" He was surprised to hear what had actually happened and that Freddie and I weren't just misbehaving again.

That choir director served continuously for more than 65 years. I told him at a celebration in his honor a few years ago, "I'm not surprised that you could last 65 years if you could put up with me!"

Freddie enjoyed pulling tricks on people. Once, as he helped his mother prepare the grape juice and bread cubes for our once–monthly communion service, Freddie added lemon juice to the grape juice.

Communion was always served to the people while seated in the pews, so I've often wondered how many of them were sprayed by surprised parishioners behind them. Unfortunately, Freddie never told me the outcome, and he passed away a few years ago. I'll just have to imagine the ending to that one.

Potatoes

Although my brother Greg is older than me, when people ask which of us is older, I tell them, "I used to be older, but then I was sick for two years." This usually brings a puzzled look for a moment, followed by laughter.

While in high school, Greg and I sometimes helped gather potatoes after they were plowed out of the ground at the family farm of our friend Gene. We were paid by the bushel, and although I don't remember how much money we made for each bushel, I know it wasn't much. Greg and I occasionally were asked to help with the sorting in the evening and we occasionally ate with the family. Meals with Gene and his family were always great feasts, and I remember one time when Gene's mother had a huge bowl of freshly made apple sauce which Greg and I nearly finished entirely on our own. Gene's mother seemed surprised, but pleased, that we enjoyed her apple sauce so much. Warm fresh apple sauce! There's nothing like it!

While picking up potatoes one day, Gene, Greg, and I were sent to the barn to get more empty bushel baskets. Gene drove an old WWII troop transport (a large jeep with a flatbed on the back). On our return trip, I sat on the tailgate with my legs dangling over the edge. Bushel baskets were stacked high on the rear of the truck bed and as we traveled up an incline on the farm lane the back row of baskets tilted rear–ward. I grabbed the stack to keep them from falling over, but the baskets toppled from the truck and so did I, landing on my backside and smacking my head on the lane. Fortunately, the lane was covered with asphalt shingle "tabs" and had a little give to it, so I wasn't hurt. Any accusation of this being the reason for my strange sense of humor cannot be proven, unless, with a time machine, the change could be discovered. After reloading the baskets onto the truck, we completed our task.

Dogs and the Friendly Fox

Dad owned hunting dogs when I was growing up, and at one time we had 13: two adult beagles, two adult foxhounds, and nine foxhound puppies. Dad often took the two adult foxhounds into the woods and let them run, hoping they would track down a fox. Sometimes they chased deer and would not come when dad called them so he sometimes came home without them. Eventually, they found their way home, usually one to three days later.

Rationing, During World War II, made it difficult or expensive to get many items, Butter included. Mom told me that during the war Dad released one of the fox hounds in the woods a few miles from home, and the next day the dog arrived at the door with a pound of butter in its mouth. I asked her if they ate it, and she said, "We sure did!" Would that make the dog a "butterhound?" I'm sure someone was very disappointed that morning, and I wonder if the delivery person and customer ever settled their differences.

Dad set traps for foxes as well, using spring loaded steel traps. To make trap "sets," he boiled the traps, wore rubber gloves and then sprinkled fox urine over the area of the trap to rid them of all human scent. Fox urine was available in some sporting goods stores but Dad decided to collect it himself. He built a wire cage divided into two compartments, with sloping corrugated tin underneath. Along the lower edge of the tin ran a gutter which drained into a bottle at the end. The first occupant was an old fox caught in a live trap, similar to the ones used for animal relocation. The second occupant was a young fox caught by a nearby farmer. Dad was now in business.

He had two foxes and was collecting some smelly stuff to help trap other foxes.

To feed the foxes, Dad occasionally got dead chickens from a nearby farm and purchased a large wheel of something like pork rinds. I enjoyed feeding the foxes, and tried to make friends with them. The old fox would have nothing to do with me and cowered in the far corner of the pen whenever I approached. The young fox, however, took food right from my hand and pressed against the cage wire to let me scratch its side and back. When I told Dad about this he said, "Stay away from the foxes. They're wild and they'll bite you." He didn't believe me, so I asked him to come with me. I took some food, gave it to the young fox through the pen wire, the young fox pressed against the cage wire and I stroked its fur. Dad said, "I'll be darned."

Scout Meeting

My parents owned four lots near the edge of a small town. We lived on one lot and farmed the other three. Across the farmed lot from our house was my neighbor and frequent playmate Brent. He and I often played in the dirt when there were no crops in that part of the field, and even had a path across it to keep from walking around the end of the field to go from one house to the other. One day Brent and I dug a large pit and short tunnel near the path crossing the field. Mom called me in and said, "I don't have time to check on you, so you have to hurry and get yourself washed so we can go to the scout meeting."

As directed, I washed my face and hands, changed clothes, and we headed off to the meeting. (This was a general meeting of parents, scouts and scout leaders.) The meeting was held in the gym/auditorium of the old town high school. The leader directed all scouts to go backstage and await further instructions while the parents found seats in the audience. The leader then told those of us behind the curtain to take off our shoes and socks and stick our feet under the curtain to see if our parents could identify us by our feet. We all lined up with our feet protruding beneath the old heavy stage curtain. After several minutes the curtain opened and every scout's mother was standing in front of her son.

My mother had no difficulty recognizing my feet immediately. Aside from the physical characteristics of my feet, there was a crusty–brown layer of dirt covering them. When I washed to go to the meeting, I didn't see any reason to wash my feet. Mom later told me she was so embarrassed that she considered not choosing me on purpose, but she really didn't have much choice. I guess it would have been pretty obvious if I was the only child not chosen and Mom was the only mother not "choosing" a son.

One Tie

Mom didn't take me shopping very often. She said I always threw a tantrum and yelled that she never bought me anything when we went shopping. She would then remind me that shelves had to be built in the attic to hold all the toys and games! On one of the rare shopping trips, she took me to get a sport coat and some slacks. After purchasing a jacket and pants, Mom asked me in front of the clerk, "Would you like to get a tie to go with your new jacket and pants?" I said, "No, I have one tie, and it goes pretty well with everything." Once again, I learned that I had embarrassed my mother immensely.

"The proverbs of Solomon: A wise son brings joy to his father, but a foolish son grief to his mother." (Proverbs 10:1)

Tractor

Dad had a Farmall Cub tractor to farm the field next to us and behind our house. I was thirteen years old when I first started driving, and the small Cub tractor was the first of many vehicles that I learned to drive. I used the tractor to disk the field in early spring or late summer or to push snow in the winter. (I couldn't plow a straight furrow, so my brother Greg did the plowing.) One time Greg drove the tractor and I rode on the draw–bar while breaking up the dirt clods with a large wooden drag. (Our "drag" was a flat platform made with heavy lumber. The front angled up to keep it from digging into the dirt as it was pulled around the field to crush the "clods" of dirt. We often put cinder blocks or large rocks on the drag to weigh it down, and sometimes I rode on it.)

The Cub tractor wouldn't start moving in third gear while pulling the drag and first or second gear was very slow. Greg decided to speed shift from second gear to third gear while moving. The plan sounded good, but when he slapped the gear shift back, it kept going. The shifting lever sailed right past me and into the dirt behind the drag. Greg hit the clutch and the brake at the same time and we came to an immediate stop. I retrieved the shift lever and after cleaning the dirt from it, Greg put it back in place and we proceeded—in second gear.

Dad was driving the tractor at another time, and I was sitting on the drag as added weight. The drag hit a large, hard dirt clod, bounced over it, and I was thrown forward. I landed between the tractor and the drag. I yelled, and thanks to Dad's quick reflexes, he stopped the tractor before the drag ran me over.

River

When I was ten years old, my family and my uncle's family went swimming in the Susquehanna River. The Susquehanna River has many islands and the water flowing around the islands and between the islands and the shore can be very swift. My uncle and brother had waded out to a large rock and were sitting on it, so Dad wanted me to wade out as well. I was standing on the bottom near the shore with an inner–tube around my body and just under my arms. Dad said it was shallow and I would have no problem walking to the boulder. I was afraid and didn't want to go, but at Dad's urging I started wading toward the boulder. As I neared the boulder, I stepped into a deep hole and it took me by surprise. I slipped through the inner–tube, losing my grip on it. As I tumbled over and over in the water, swept away by the current, I began screaming. Of course with each breath I was only getting water in my lungs. I came up once, then twice, and when I surfaced the third time, my uncle grabbed me and brought me to the boulder. I remember sitting on the boulder crying, choking and coughing. If my uncle hadn't been there that day, I wouldn't be writing this.

Later that year, I developed an extremely bad case of bronchitis, no doubt from having so much water in my lungs. I remember at the beginning of sixth grade, I could not run or play. Anything that made me breathe deeply caused me to cough until I vomited.

The bronchitis cleared up during that school year, and I've had no lasting effects from it. In fact, during my tenth grade health class we conducted an experiment to measure lung capacity. First, a washbowl was half filled with water, then a water filled bell jar was placed upside down in the bowl so that the mouth of the jar was under the water in the bowl. A hose was then inserted under the mouth of the jar and one–by–one, the students took a deep breath and blew air through the hose, into the jar, to see how much water could be displaced. Out of the entire class, I was the only one who could empty the bell jar. God not only restores, but He makes things better than new!

"Praise the Lord, O my soul; all my inmost being, praise his holy name. Praise the Lord, O my soul, and forget not all his benefits – who forgives all your sins and heals all your diseases, who redeems your life from the pit and crowns you with love and compassion, who satisfies your desires with good things so that your youth is renewed like the eagle's." (Psalm 103:1–5)

"From inside the fish Jonah prayed to the Lord his God. He said: 'In my distress I called to the Lord, and he answered me. From the depths of the grave I called for help, and you listened to my cry. You hurled me into the deep, into the very heart of the seas, and the currents swirled about me; all your waves and breakers swept over me.' I said, 'I have been banished from your sight; yet I will look again toward your holy temple.' The engulfing waters threatened me, the deep surrounded me; seaweed was wrapped around my head. To the roots of the mountains I sank down; the earth beneath barred me in forever. But you brought my life up from the pit, O Lord my God. When my life was ebbing away, I remembered you, Lord, and my prayer rose to you, to your holy temple. Those who cling to worthless idols forfeit the grace that could be theirs. But I, with a song of thanksgiving, will sacrifice to you. What I

have vowed, I will make good. Salvation comes from the Lord." (Jonah 2:1–9)

School Bus Bump

In sixth grade, I was assigned to a school several miles from my home. This was the only year I was not within walking distance of school. During this time, road crews were re–surfacing a portion of the road that we traveled, and a four inch difference in surface level caused quite an interesting opportunity. A few friends and I sat in the rear of the bus, flexed our knees and leaned slightly forward (as though we were going to stand up). When the rear tires of the bus hit the bump we were airborne! One day I either flexed too much or the bump was worse, but I bounced so high that I hit my head on the roof of the school bus. I hit the seat hard enough on my way down to consider that my spanking and I never did *that* again. I was very fortunate to sustain no injuries.

Home Made Rocket Fuel

Dave was a new kid in school. He moved into an old farmhouse down the road a half mile or so from where I lived, an easy bike ride away. He was cool. He enjoyed experimenting, electronics and other activities that I enjoyed. We dissected small transformers (electrical transformers used to convert voltages, not the toys that convert from robots to other things) to remove the hair–sized wire that made up the coils and used the wires for various projects. One time Dave used the thin wire for a dangerous experiment. He stretched several yards of the wire on the rug in his bedroom—in serpentine fashion—and then stuck the ends into the electrical socket. The wire immediately became red hot and vaporized, leaving a black line in its place. Not only did he ruin an expensive woven rug, he could have started a fire! His parents were very lenient, but he didn't get away unscathed with that one; he was grounded for a while.

Dave and I made rocket fuel (similar to a gunpowder recipe). We wrapped the fuel in aluminum foil, shaped it to look like a rocket—complete with fins—and put a fuse in the tail end. We placed our homemade rocket on the main road in front of Dave's house, lit the fuse and ran a safe distance away to watch. The "rocket" didn't move much, but it sure did put out a thick cloud of noxious gas! The cloud drifted over the road like fog on a late October morning, and traffic (what little there was) came to a complete stop. Unfortunately, my dad drove by just in time to see the cloud rolling across the street. I was concerned about his reaction, but he didn't say much, other than to suggest that we not do that again.

The Last Rocket Fuel

After successfully making "rocket fuel" with Dave and my neighbor Brent, I was pretty confident and thought I could do a better job. I was alone in our kitchen where I mixed the ingredients, adding water and stirring until it became a paste. I held a metal jar lid, containing the mixture, by a pair of pliers in my left hand. Then I "cooked" the mixture over a lit candle until almost all of the water was gone and the mixture was pretty solid. Unfortunately, the mixture got too hot, ignited, and severely burned 3 fingers on my left hand. Large blisters formed on my middle, ring and little fingers.

Our family doctor lived and had his practice in the next town. He made house calls, but money was pretty tight. The next day I noticed him entering our neighbor's house and told Mom. She told me to watch for him to come out of the house and then quickly run and show him my hand. I did what Mom told me, and when I showed him the blisters he told me to put "Good Samaritan Salve" on the burned areas, but otherwise do nothing. (Good Samaritan Salve was a wonderful beige paste in a red and white tin, and was used for everything from skin eruptions and infections to drawing out splinters. Nothing I have found over the years comes close to the effectiveness of that product!) I followed his advice and my fingers healed without any scars or indication of injury.

Bicycle Riding

My worst bicycle accident occurred when I thought I was good enough to try some tricks. One trick was an attempt to reverse the steering instructions in my brain. I crossed my arms, placing the left hand on the right handlebar, and the right hand on the left handlebar. It seemed simple, but I jerked the handlebars to one side to make a course correction, and it was the wrong direction, and I flew over the handlebars onto the road. I never tried that again. (Reactions are faster than thoughts!) *"Pride goes before destruction, a haughty spirit before a fall."* (Proverbs 16:18)

In the summer after sixth grade, a friend and I decided to ride our bicycles to the home of our school bus driver, who we had grown to like during the school year. He lived about 15 miles north of us, so we rode our bikes on the expressway, which was under construction at the time. After our visit, we rode home, stopping along the way at one of the construction sites for some water. We were very warm from riding in the hot summer sun, so we drank a lot of ice–cold water.

After arriving home, I got quite sick and later realized that it was heat stroke! I was sunburned and overheated, and the ice–cold water had been too much: another of life's lessons learned!

Golf Ball Bat

Everyone knows that you hit baseballs with bats, and golf balls with clubs (golf clubs that is). When my neighbor Brent and I were young (old enough to know better, though), we decided to change things around a bit. Brent said, "how far do you think a golf ball will go if you hit it with a baseball bat?" Well, I had no idea. I wasn't interested in baseball or golf (or any sport for that matter). So, as we stood in the back yard of the fifth house down the street from my house, Brent tossed a golf ball into the air, wound up and smacked it. I was quite impressed with the trajectory and speed of that golf ball!

Approximately one hundred feet behind my house sat a cinder block garage used to store a truck, tractor and implements for the tractor. A large picture window in the side of the garage faced the direction of the hit golf ball. As I watched the arc of the golf ball I suddenly realized the possible outcome. Brent and I held our breath as the ball struck the cinder block wall, narrowly missing the picture window by only a few inches.

We now knew that a golf ball, hit by a bat, travels quite far. I'm surprised that this variation of golf never caught on. I think there might be some merit to a tournament using a baseball bat in place of the variety of clubs. It sure would make the game simpler and eliminate the need for a whole bag of equipment. One baseball bat and one putter. (Ok, maybe one sand wedge as well.)

Boxing

Brent was four months older than me and was always better at sports. I remember one day in my attic Brent and I were trying out some new boxing gloves. Brent was pretty good, and I was doing my best to fend off his advances. Suddenly, he saw an opening and landed a particularly good (and hard) punch on the side of my face. Down I went, eyes closed and not moving. I was out cold. Brent took off running and didn't stop until he was home. Mom, hearing the commotion (and no doubt hearing Brent's fast exit), came to the attic to see what was going on, found me lying on the floor and revived me. When I talked to Brent later, he said he ran because he thought he had killed me, and didn't want to face my mother.

Gunpowder and Sulfur

One of our calmer adventures got Brent and me in serious trouble with our parents. My dad enjoyed reloading his own ammunition so he had several cans of gunpowder on hand at all times. One day Brent and I took some of the gunpowder and poured it out on the cement just off his back porch, where the old well and hand pump had been. We made patterns—our initials etc.—and then lit one end of the powder. We enjoyed watching it burn, following the patterns we had created. Unfortunately, the burn marks were permanent, so Brent got in trouble for putting graffiti on the cement and I got in trouble for getting into Dad's gunpowder.

Another time, we obtained a good supply of sulfur, and Brent wanted to see how well it would burn by itself. We were in his basement at the time. The basement windows were "tilt–in" metal frames with two panes of glass. We had no idea how much odor is created by burning sulfur, nor how much smoke is produced by such a slow burning substance. Burning sulfur has a particularly bad smell, not unlike rotten eggs. I think Brent's family left the basement windows open for a week or two after that, and Brent and I couldn't see each other for a while. (I just realized why it seems like I didn't see Brent all that much when we were growing up.)

Fireworks

Brent and I always had some sort of fireworks when we were growing up (one inch and two inch salutes, cherry bombs, and my favorite—lady fingers), and there were ample remote areas to set them off. One of our favorite activities was to line up plastic army men, trucks, tanks, etc., then put salutes into the dirt and detonate them, propelling men and machines into the air. The scenes looked pretty real (except without blood—unless we held on to the salute too long on the "grenade toss").

Once while setting off salutes after dark, Brent held a salute behind his head (as though he was going to throw a football) while I tried to light the fuse. Paper fuses didn't light evenly, and sometimes the paper smoldered, but nothing happened until the powder caught fire. Then it would go like gang–busters! On this occasion Brent hesitated just a little too long or the powder took off without warning because, just as he was throwing it, the salute exploded in his fingers. Brent said he couldn't feel his fingers, so we quickly ran to a street light to see if his fingers were still attached. They were. We were very glad it wasn't a cherry bomb or an M–80 that he was throwing.

Of course, the cherry bombs and M–80s had better fuses. In fact, we enjoyed demonstrating how fuses burn under water. We tied a cherry bomb or M–80 to a rock, lit the fuse and threw it into a pond. The bomb gave a muffled "Wump!" followed by bubbles. Sometimes a sunfish surfaced with the bubbles. (This warning may be a bit late in the book, but parents should use caution in allowing youngsters to read these stories!)

The End of Morse Code

I have been interested in electronics since childhood. Early in my teens I learned Morse code, and when I was fifteen I received my first Ham (Amateur Radio) license. My neighbor Brent was interested in sports and wasn't too keen on all that "technical stuff," but somehow I convinced him to let me run a wire across the open field between our houses (during the winter), and communicate using a telegraph key and buzzer. This was a great way for us to practice. One day, we were taking turns sending messages back and forth (we both sent very slowly and then had to throw a switch to allow the other person to send), and I had to go to the bathroom. Brent was sending and I could do nothing until he finished. By the time I could send him a message I was desperate. Trying to save time, I simply sent: M–U–S–T S–H–I–T. I dashed off to the bathroom and didn't think any more of it. When I returned to the telegraph key, I couldn't get a response from Brent. He told me later that his dad chose that moment to read what he was printing, signaling the end of the communication link between our houses. Brent never did learn Morse Code. I learned that I must compose my messages with more forethought, even in an emergency. I did continue on and received my first of three Amateur Radio Licenses in 1960.

Dr. Pepper

American Bandstand was all the rage when I was in high school. TV stations around the country relayed the broadcast from Philadelphia, Pennsylvania. Many local TV stations even emulated the popular dance show. WGAL–TV in Lancaster, Pennsylvania was one of them. The station invited high schools around the area to participate, one school at a time. Eventually, it was my high school's turn.

I've never been a good dancer, even in high school. Rhythm was never one of my talents. I enjoyed slow dancing, but when the songs were fast I usually excused myself and moved to a spot far from the dance floor. Nevertheless, when our high school was given the opportunity to participate in the TV studio dance, I decided to go with my classmates.

Just as they do now, sponsors paid for programming in order to promote their product, and this show was no different. Dr. Pepper was a new taste (at least to me) and the show's main provider. Off to one side of the dance floor sat a cooler filled with Dr. Pepper for the dancers. Between songs, the host of the show walked around with a microphone asking the dancers how they liked the taste of Dr. Pepper. Every time I saw him heading my way, I walked the other way to escape. That is, until he surprised me when I wasn't looking.

TV Broadcasts in the late 50's and early 60's were live. Mistakes were broadcast as they happened. When the host of the show caught me unaware, he quickly said, "And you sir, what do you think of the new taste of Dr. Pepper?" When he shoved the microphone in my face, I honestly replied, "I don't really like it." He jerked the microphone away from my mouth, wheeled around and hurried to the next closest person. I realized that I had been just a little too honest in my appraisal of the product. I later came to like Dr. Pepper, and have since regretted my quick response to the announcer's question. Still, it probably gave viewers a good chuckle.

Itch

A large (and mostly overgrown) nursery existed directly across from my neighbor Brent's house. A group of boys, including Brent and myself, often went through the nursery, across some railroad tracks and up into wooded hills to wander around. During these outings, nature calls required improvisation. On one such occasion, I found a good spot on a log and extended my backside over it. We all know that no job is complete until the paperwork is done, but having no paper, I grabbed some leaves.

My choice of leaves was unfortunate, as I ended up with poison ivy in places that just weren't appropriate for scratching in public. Sitting on hard wooden chairs in school didn't help one bit, and I had an especially difficult time sitting still in class. One of my teachers was quite versed in Pennsylvania Dutch, and kept saying, "Quit your rutching!" (It actually sounded like, "Quitchurrutchin")

In time, the itching went away, but I never tried replacing toilet paper with leaves again. I learned many things while young, but some lessons are really memorable.

Weight Lifting

Dad made a set of barbells and weights from surplus iron around the end of World War II, which worked almost as well as store–bought weights. The only problem was with the screw on the end piece that held the "disk weights" onto the bar. It was impossible to tighten, which allowed the weights to slip off when the bar was tilted. One time while lifting weights in the basement I tipped it too much, allowing one of the weights to slide off. The weight hit the painted cement floor chipping the cement and leaving an obvious white mark in the grey painted floor. Not knowing what else to do, I put a small piece of black electrical tape on the white patch of cement. (Dad wouldn't notice black on grey, right?) The next day Dad asked me, "who put the piece of electrical tape on the basement floor to cover up the chipped spot?" Busted!

High School High Jinx

During my sophomore year in high school, I was a member of the "stage crew club." My duties included operating the curtain during plays, operating the lighting or sound equipment, and showing movies during school assemblies. One day I was assigned to operate the carbon arc movie projector and house lighting for a junior high class science assembly and so I was located in the projection booth high in the rear of the auditorium. Once the movie was rolling, I took the opportunity to cross a steel catwalk that ran above the auditorium ceiling, from the projection booth to the backstage area in the front of the auditorium to have a cigarette. All went well until I encountered a huge metal air conditioning duct approximately half way there. The duct was too large to just step over and as I put some of my weight on it to swing my leg over, the sheet metal flexed making a loud "KA–BOOM" sound. As I lifted my weight off the duct, it un–flexed, and another "KA–BOOM" sounded. Of course, on the way back after enjoying a quick cigarette backstage, I had the same problem. The science teacher, who was quite hard–of–hearing, approached me after the assembly to ask, "What was going on upstairs? It sounded like mice walking around." I just laughed because the students said it sounded like thunder.

Mixing Chemicals

The following year I wanted to try something different and so I joined the photography club. I enjoyed this club much more than the stage crew club and still use the skills I learned those many years ago. Although I now use digital cameras that are capable of doing everything automatically, I learned to take photographs with a Graflex Speed Graphic 4x5 sheet film camera. It might as well have been the 30's or 40's instead of the 60's. The camera can be seen in the old black and white movies. The camera may have been old (or old technology), but it took great pictures and taught me a great deal about photography.

The photography club was responsible for all of the school activity pictures for the yearbook. Although I took some of the photos, the majority were taken by club members with more experience, usually a second or third year member. As a first year member, I needed experience in all areas of photography, including developing and printing. So one day the teacher in charge of the club asked me to mix the chemicals for developing film by following the written directions posted on the cabinet in the dark room. I found everything as he told me and began mixing the chemicals, placing the finished solution into the developer bottle. A few days later, the teacher asked me how I had mixed the chemicals, so I explained each step that I followed. When I finished describing the procedure that I had followed, he calmly, but firmly, explained that *two* sets of instructions were on that paper, separated by one blank line. The first procedure was for mixing the developer and the second was for the "fixer" solution. (fixer is used to stop or neutralize the developer process) The teacher went on to say that several photos from a basketball game were ruined by the developer/fixer mixture. I later learned how to mix the chemicals properly, and went on to develop and print my own photographs. This was a stepping stone to my lifelong enjoyment of photography and videography.

Water and Gas

One practical joke, in which I was not involved, took place in the science lab of my high school. I heard the story immediately after it happened so I'm sure it is true. The science lab room was well–equipped with water and gas outlets at several stations along the workbenches. Tubing was used to connect the water line or gas line to lab equipment for experiments. The tubing was interchangeable, as the water and gas outlets had the same tapered ends, with ridges to hold the tubing in place.

Before class one day, a student (I knew who it was at the time) connected the gas line to the water line and turned them both on. The water line had about twenty pounds per Square inch (PSI) of pressure and the gas line had only five PSI. This caused water (greater pressure) to enter the gas line. Both valves were opened for several seconds and then closed. The tubing was then removed and put away.

When the teacher arrived and class began, students were directed to set up Bunsen burners, one for each pair of students. With lighters in hand, the students were ready to ignite the gas at the direction of the teacher. When given the signal to begin, rather than gas coming out of the burner, water shot into the air! Each Bunsen burner became a fountain!

Have you ever wondered why water doesn't burn? Water is composed of Hydrogen and Oxygen. Hydrogen is extremely flammable, especially when there is Oxygen present. Yet, we use water to put out fires! God is awesome and I believe He has a sense of humor! (I bet He thought... "Let man try to figure this one out!") *"Sing to the LORD, all the earth; proclaim his salvation day after day. Declare his glory among the nations, his marvelous deeds among all peoples. For great is the LORD and most worthy of praise; he is to be feared above all gods. For all the gods of the nations are idols, but the LORD made the heavens."* (1Chronicles 16:23–26)

Flying Chicken

Anyone familiar with chickens (or has seen the movie Chicken Run), knows that chickens can't fly. At least not without help. Wally was a high school friend and a year younger than me. He drove a 1930's coupe that his dad bought for him. He was very fond of the old car. I, too, thought the car was really cool. Wally had just gotten his driver's license and was not very comfortable navigating back country roads. When his parents invited us to visit their lakeside bungalow, Wally asked me to drive his car. We traveled many back roads, and traffic was sparse. We finally came to a fairly straight stretch of road even though it was quite hilly, so Wally said, "Open it up and let's see what it'll do!" I asked, "Are you sure?" "Yes," he said.

As we crested the next hill, I "put the pedal to the metal!" Now this wasn't one of those souped–up hot–rods, but since we were already heading downhill, we picked up quite a bit of speed. At the bottom of the hill, on the right, was an old house that looked like Jed Clampett's original home—before they moved to Beverly Hills in the TV series "The Beverly Hillbillies." In the front yard of the old house were several chickens. The chickens got very excited as we approached and all of them began running around like a chicken with its head cut off. (Fast, blindly, and in no particular direction.) One even tried to cross the road. (*Why do they do that?*) When the road–crossing chicken realized a large object was gathering speed toward it, the chicken decided to fly. Now, as I stated earlier; chickens can't fly. Maybe they could fly at one time and forgot how. It certainly seems to be a reflex action. Their desire to fly is obvious at times like this, and the willingness to try is apparent. However, this chicken in its excitement, achieved only enough altitude to make contact with the rounded, front right fender of the old coupe. With the added help from the fender, that bird flew! It wasn't one of those graceful flights of a "real" bird. It was more like a shot put arc. But that bird none–the–less made it back into the yard from whence it came (condition unknown), and probably set a new flight distance record for the species.

"but those who hope in the LORD will renew their strength. They will soar on wings like eagles; they will run and not grow weary, they will walk and not be faint." (Isaiah 40:31)

Same Voices

We had one telephone in the house when I was young, and whoever was nearest the phone when it rang, answered it. In my later teens, my dad, my brother, and I, could not be distinguished on the telephone. This occasionally caused some confusion. For instance, when my brother's date from the previous evening called, she started right in with, "I just wanted to thank you for last night, and...." I broke in and said, "Hold on, this is Robert. I'll get Greg for you." Maybe I shouldn't have done that. Who knows what I might have found out? Then again, I think it was the right decision. I would have been caught and two people would have been angry at me.

Fishing

Chuck was a friend through our mutual enjoyment of Ham Radio and his parents had a bungalow along the Susquehanna River that he wanted me to see. He gave me directions and I met him there. After showing me around the property, we both got into my VW Beetle and drove a little further down the river to go fishing. Worms have never been my choice for bait as they are slippery, wiggly, and difficult to put on a hook or keep on the hook while casting. I prefer to use corn, which is much easier to work with and even more plentiful. For this reason, I brought a can of corn with me. I opened the lid half way, with a "K–rations" can opener that I kept on my key ring, as I wanted to be able to hinge the lid and keep the rest of the corn from spilling out after using what I needed. Using my car key for leverage, I attempted to pry the lid up enough to get some corn out of the can. To my horror, the key immediately snapped in two! Let's see: aluminum key, steel (tin) can lid. I should have known what would happen. I now had no key with which to drive my car home! Fortunately, the car was open, so we stored our fishing gear in it while we walked back to the bungalow to get Chuck's firebird.

Chuck said he could push my car with his car. The idea sounded good, but my car's steering column locked when the key was not in the ignition. I tried turning the wheel and found that with a great deal of effort I could force the wheel past the locked position by jerking it sharply. This made steering very erratic, but it could be done.

Chuck pulled his car behind mine and began pushing slowly, as I jerked the wheel sharply in the direction I needed to go. We were only five miles from home and on back roads until we passed through two small towns about two miles from my house. Traffic was very light, and other than the sharp left or right turns that required me to grip the steering wheel in both hands and jerk it as hard as I could to overcome the "stops" in the steering mechanism, the trip went well. Chuck was careful to follow my erratic arcs on the turns and kept his car against my rear bumper as much as he could. He also had to allow me to drift to stop signs then slowly begin pushing me again. When we made the final turn into my driveway, I could finally relax. I immediately borrowed my dad's car and drove to a key shop to secure a new key (and a spare). The journey taught me two more of life's lessons: car keys do not make good prying tools, and *always* keep a spare key with you.

Angus

During the summer following High School graduation, a classmate of mine told me she knew a young man named Harvey who needed a driver. When I inquired about the job, I learned that Harvey had been caught speeding too many times, and his license had been suspended for 30 days. Harvey worked for an artificial cattle–breeding service and traveled to remote farms, averaging about 100 miles per day. Harvey hired me as his driver, which proved to be an interesting experience.

Because Harvey could not drive, he allowed me to take his car home with me. Each day I packed my lunch, drove a few miles to pick him up, then we headed to his "office" (a room in a local farmer's market) to pick up the "materials" for his job.

Harvey and I spent all day on the road, so we took our lunch break whenever and wherever we could. I suspect some people might have trouble eating with some of the aromas that we occasionally endured during our lunches in or near the barns. Believe me, we got used to it.

Bathroom facilities were sparse on the open road, and some of the barns we visited were not located near the farm house. We relieved ourselves behind the barn or wherever we could. Once, while searching for just such a spot, I found myself feeling my way along the cattle stalls in the lower level of a barn that had been built into a hillside, making the lower level pitch black, at least until the eyes could adjust to the near darkness. I rounded the stall partition into what I thought was an empty stall and began relieving myself. As my eyes slowly adjusted to the darkness, I became aware of a huge dark shape next to me. As I began to make out the shape, I was startled. I had walked into a stall between the stall divider and a very large Black Angus bull! The bull probably weighed over one thousand pounds, and could easily have crushed me against the side of the stall. Why he stood there absolutely quiet and allowed me to use his stall as a urinal still amazes me after all these years. That was one job I left unfinished, feeling that retreat was more important than total relief.

At another farm, I stayed at the barn while Harvey went with the farmer to the house. As I waited, a very large hornet kept circling around me. Lying on the ground nearby was a two–by–four about the length of a baseball bat. I picked up the lumber and smacked the hornet into oblivion. It was a perfect hit and would have been at least a double in any ball game. Within seconds after dispatching the first hornet there were four or five more large hornets buzzing around me. I dropped the "bat" and made a fast dash to the farm house, where I got some rather startled looks as I burst through the front door. Once I explained the reason for my sudden intrusion, everyone had a good laugh.

While Harvey and I traveled the back roads of rural Pennsylvania, we saw many handwritten signs advertising items such as produce and animals. One day we passed a sign which consisted of a jagged piece of weathered board mostly painted white and roughly hand lettered in black. The sign stated, "Fresh Heifer for Sale." In dairy farm jargon, "fresh" means a cow that has recently given birth, and has begun giving milk. (or the milk supply has increased if she was already giving milk) "Heifer" is a cow that has never given birth. I can only guess that the farmer meant that the cow had given birth for the first time. Harvey and I had a good laugh over that sign.

Because we traveled mostly on back country roads, we rarely encountered other cars. One time however, as we approached a one–lane bridge, a car was approaching the bridge from the other end. Since he was farther from the bridge than we were, I started to drive across. The other driver suddenly gunned the engine and sped onto the bridge. We passed each other near his end of the bridge and just as he passed me, I heard a loud scraping noise, but Harvey and I didn't feel anything. I looked in the rearview mirror and saw sparks flying from under the other car. He had hit the joint at the bridge entrance hard enough to jar his muffler and tailpipe loose, causing them to fall and drag on the pavement just as our cars passed. Harvey and I both laughed and agreed that he deserved it. Harvey said he knew I was a good driver, but he was amazed that we were able to pass on a "one lane bridge!" (I was amazed too!) *"The arrogance of man will be brought low and the pride of men humbled; the LORD alone will be exalted in that day, and the idols will totally disappear."* (Isaiah 2:17–18)

JFK

Penn State College has campuses in various locations, and one of those happened to be in York, Pennsylvania, a short distance from where I was born and raised. After graduating from high school, I entered school there and at the same time, through a friend, got a job at the local TV station as a cameraman.

On the twenty second of November, while attending class on campus, we were interrupted by the Dean of the school, telling us that President Kennedy had been shot in Dallas, and classes were cancelled for the day. The campus was not far from the TV station, so I drove there and spent the rest of the day watching the network link in the control room. There are several days in my life that I will never forget, and this was one of them.

Hospital

Hernia

My heart wasn't really into college right out of high school. Dad suggested I might try enlisting in the military. (With the draft system in place and my not continuing in school, it was pretty certain I would be going that direction anyway.) So I planned to enlist in the United States Air Force (USAF). During the physical examination, the doctor discovered a hernia. The Air Force rejected me for medical reasons. They told me the Army would draft me and then operate, but the USAF didn't want me. (I should have known that wasn't true.) Dad suggested that I have the hernia repaired while I was young, because it would just get worse as I got older. I knew I had a lump on the lower right side of my abdomen from being hit by a baseball when I was about 12, but I didn't know it was a hernia.

The operation led to my very first hospital visit. After the preliminary paperwork, blood taking, temperature taking and blood pressure checking, I was shown to my room and told to change into a small gown, removing even my underwear. This was my first experience with a hospital gown. It didn't quite come down to my knees and was supposed to tie in the back, but I didn't bother tying it as it didn't cover much anyway. I just hopped into bed and pulled the sheet over me. Shortly after I was in bed, two people entered my room, one behind the other. The first was a young, short, blond woman, who looked to be about 24 years old and was quite pretty. Behind her was a tall older man who had a bit of silver in his hair. They both walked to my bed–side. Without saying a word to me more than "hello," the young woman pulled the sheet down, pulled my gown up and began talking to the man accompanying her. After possibly noticing the shear panic on my face, she said to me, "Oh, I'm your surgeon. This is your anesthesiologist." She continued explaining the surgery to the man with her, and then they both left.

They could have done a bit more introduction *before* the unveiling as far as I was concerned!

Later that evening, I slipped out of bed to retrieve a cigarette from my shirt lying on the chair across the room. As I bent over to remove the pack of cigarettes from the shirt pocket, my gown fell forward, leaving nothing to the imagination from the aft side. After accomplishing my mission, I turned and looked behind me to discover that the door to my room was open and lined up perfectly with the door to the room across the hall, which was also open. In the room across the hall, were two elderly lady visitors staring at me. Their eyes were open wide. I do believe they were grinning! Embarrassed, I quickly returned to bed and covered up with the sheet. I certainly hadn't intended to "moon" the old ladies!

In the morning, a nursing student arrived, carrying an old–fashioned, rubber water bottle with a long tube hanging out of it. I knew this was not a good sign. She said she needed to give me an enema. She was trying to be very professional, talking about other things as she went about completing her "task." Since I looked rather young for my age, she assumed that I was in school, and commented about my getting a break from school. When she discovered that we were the same age, she became rather quiet, not knowing what else to say. This was an experience I hoped wouldn't be repeated, and I could tell that she wasn't anxious to repeat it either. I suspect she drew the short straw that day, or perhaps every nursing student must experience that job. I wasn't sure I would make the trip to the bathroom in time, but in the end, everything came out well.

In the 60's, I suppose Sodium Pentothal was the anesthesia medicine of choice, since this is what I was given for this operation. After the surgery, I kept falling asleep, drifting in and out of consciousness. I needed to choose lunch items from a menu, but not being fully "with it" even when awake, the only two things that looked good were spinach and Jell–O. Mom was visiting when the food arrived and when she saw what I had chosen, she rounded up a nurse and talked her into getting me a small chicken pot pie. Although I love both spinach and Jell–O, I never enjoyed chicken pot–pie more. I had a bigger appetite once the anesthesia wore off.

After complete healing, I successfully entered and served four years in the USAF.

Wisdom Teeth

In 1968, after being discharged from the USAF, my dentist discovered I had impacted wisdom teeth, and referred me to an oral surgeon to have them removed. A couple of days after meeting the surgeon and scheduling the operation, while visiting a family that I knew (in a very small nearby town), the oral surgeon also came to visit the family. It turned out that the two girls in the family were the surgeon's baby–sitters!

When he entered and saw me there, he became terribly embarrassed because he had a bad case of the hiccups! He just kept apologizing over and over. He must have thought I would worry about his ability to be steady during the surgery, but that thought never entered my mind.

The day before the surgery, I was checked into the hospital and after the normal battery of tests, I slept as best I could in a hospital room. I never did figure out why they come in at midnight and wake you up to give you a sleeping pill!

The following morning a nurse and an orderly arrived to wheel me to the operating room. The nurse gave me a shot to start drying out my mouth and relax me and then I was transferred from the bed to a gurney for the trip to the operating room. Parking the gurney next to the operating table, they then had me move onto the operating table and lie on my back. The operating room nurse asked me sit up temporarily while she placed a board part way under the left side of the thin mat on the operating table. This board was approximately eight inches wide and not very thick, with most of it extending away from the operating table. She explained that the board was necessary to lay my arm on, so the anesthetic could be intravenously applied. When she put the board under me and I lay back down, my arm reached beyond the end of the board. She apologized and said, "My, you have long arms, I need to have you sit up again so I can pull the board out some more." I said, "That's from swinging in trees." She laughed and said no one had ever come to the operating room with a sense of humor! (I bet that gave them something to talk about for a while in the O.R.) The nurse then inserted the needle into my arm for the anesthesia and told me to count backwards from ten to one. When I got to one, I stopped and lay there quietly. The nurse went about getting things ready for surgery, walking back and forth in the room. I was looking around the room with my eyes, not wanting to move and disrupt anything. I admired the old wood and glass cabinets on the wall. The hospital was quite old and the craftsmanship of the old cabinets was apparent. When the nurse came near me again, I turned my head to ask her a question and she jumped back about two feet! She said, "I thought you were 'out'!" "Nope," I said, "just didn't have anything to say!" She laughed again. I soon felt as though a curtain was being lowered over my eyes. I said "OK, here I go!" The next thing I knew, I was back in my room. The surgeon warned me that I would look like a chipmunk for a while after the operation, but I had no swelling whatsoever! I suspect he performed the operation extra carefully because of the hiccup incident.

Chapter II: Military and Beyond

Army

In April 1964, I enlisted in the United States Air Force. My paternal grandmother never did figure out the difference between the army and the air force. To her, any military branch was "the army." Although she died during the second year of my enlistment, I told her several times that I was not in the army; I was in the air force. Nevertheless, every time I came home (which was pretty often while I was stationed on the east coast) she asked me how the army was. After she died, I realized that it really didn't matter whether it was the army or the air force. Funny how little things can be so annoying when someone is with us and so meaningless when they are not.

"Blessed is the man who finds wisdom, the man who gains understanding, for she is more profitable than silver and yields better returns than gold. She is more precious than rubies; nothing you desire can compare with her." (Proverbs 3:13-15)

Korat (Nakhon Ratchasima), Thailand

Perhaps I should explain how I happened to be on the other side of the world for part of my Air Force experience.

From Basic training at Lackland Air Force Base Near San Antonio, Texas, I was sent with a group of Airmen to Keesler Air Force Base in Biloxi, Mississippi to attend classes in aircraft communication equipment. (Training in electronic basics and specific communications gear)

After approximately one year at Keesler AFB and having completed the necessary training, a small group of us were sent to McGuire AFB in New Jersey, where we began working on cargo aircraft, such as the C–130 and C–135, among others. Several months later, we were told that we had been selected to be trained on the F–105 aircraft, and would be sent to Southeast Asia under a program called: "Operation Limelight." This was to be a secret operation (the official government position at this time was, "We are NOT in Vietnam."), and we weren't to tell anyone where we were going.

After initial training at McConnell AFB in Kansas, we were told to take leave, and orders would be arriving at our homes for the next phase of our deployment.

Orders did not arrive in a timely manner, so I contacted the personnel department. I was told that orders should be received shortly. Another several days went by. No orders. Again I called the personnel department. Orders would be sent shortly. Finally, orders arrived, but only stating that I should report to Edwards AFB in California. I thought this was strange, but I packed my military bag and flew to Edwards AFB, California.

The day after arriving at Edwards AFB, I visited with the personnel department and inquired about further orders. They had nothing but would check. (they seemed baffled as to why I was there, and why my orders stated nothing but "report to Edwards AFB.")

After 3 days of bugging the folks in the personnel office, I was given orders to report to Kadina AFB, Okinawa, where I finally met up with the rest of my group. We actually spent the next two–and–a–half months in Okinawa before finally being sent to Korat, Thailand.

Rescue Helicopter Ride

I spent nine–and–a–half months in Korat, Thailand from 1966 to 1967, working in the aircraft radio shop and on the flight line. Although I never tired of watching the F–105

fly, I had no desire to ride in one. (Most were single seat aircraft, but we did have a few "D" models, which had two seats) I would get sick just riding roller coasters and the "Mad Hatter's Tea Cup" rides at a fair or carnival.

Often, I observed a helicopter flying around the base however, and thought it was much more my speed. One morning I asked the helicopter pilot if I could get a ride and he agreed to take me along on a training flight that afternoon.

At the appointed time, I grabbed my camera and several rolls of film, then rode my bicycle from the "hootch" (what the barracks were called in Thailand) to the flight line. The helicopter was a twin (intertwined) blade "HH43" Rescue Helicopter. The helicopter body was short and stubby with large doors on both sides (to get a stretcher in/out), and a large opening in the rear. The rear opening had a cargo net (netting made out of wide webbing material) stretched across it, but the side doorways were unobstructed. This seemed to be the perfect platform from which to take aerial photos.

We took off and as we circled the base, I began snapping pictures. The view was fantastic. We soon began to descend. I was a little curious about our short flight. As we glided toward the runway, the engine power was reduced severely. We touched down on the runway, rolled a little, and stopped. After a brief pause, the engine roared to full power and we rose quickly, banking steeply to the right. I again began taking photos. Soon I felt the helicopter banking very steeply and descending rapidly, but with full power. I looked up to see what was going on, and discovered that we were making a mock "strafing run" at the base dump where a few trucks were in the process of dumping their loads. The Thai truck drivers were running for cover behind their trucks! The Thai truck drivers must have thought the Americans had lost their minds!

After a few more up, down, and around maneuvers, I asked the crew chief (the only person in the back with me) why the pilot was doing these "touch–and–go" maneuvers. He explained that they were practicing "power off" landings. I always thought power off meant straight down for a helicopter, but I discovered this helicopter was designed to "auto–gyro" and provide enough lift to have a controlled landing, if you can approach at the proper glide angle. (Straight down is NOT an option.)

After finishing one roll of film, I turned my full attention to reloading the camera. When I glanced out the side door opposite me, all I could see was sky—no horizon. When I looked out of the nearest doorway, all I saw was the ground. I looked out the back of the helicopter and the horizon was vertical; but I had no sensation of turning, falling, or being other than horizontal. With all the touch–and–go, circling, and now the confusion in my mind, I was ready for the flight to end. I was at the mercy of the training schedule, however, and remained on board a while longer.

Eventually the ride ended. I gathered my camera equipment, exited the helicopter—staggering—and tried to ride my bike back to the "hootch," but I didn't have enough equilibrium to ride! I walked my bike all the way and I'm sure if anyone saw me, they thought I was drunk. After finally reaching my bunk, I laid down with one foot on the floor, watching the ceiling go round and round. I never again asked for a ride on one of those "gentle" helicopters!

Cheng Mei

Cheng Mei, in the north–western corner of Thailand, is a fairly remote tourist attraction, but is visited by people from around the world. A friend and I scheduled a three day pass so we could visit the city. The base I was assigned to offered occasional flights for R&R purposes (Rest and Relaxation), so we made the necessary arrangements, packed our bags and boarded an old C–47 "tail dragger" for the flight to Cheng Mei.

A few times during the flight, the pilot or navigator walked back to the middle of the airplane and peered out the left side at the engine. I wasn't too concerned, but just a little curious about the attention paid to that engine. I peered out the small oval window and noted the oil streaked, dented, loose sheet metal that made up the cowling and cover of the engine. The engines and every other part of the airplane had seen many years of service. (The C–47 was built in or about 1942, so the aircraft was approximately 24 years old at this time) It had obviously seen hard service.

The flight was uneventful, and after quickly checking into a hotel and exchanging our uniforms for civilian clothes, we began touring the city. Our first stop was a woodcarving factory. (Every type of artistry shop was called a factory, probably because of the language difference. Most places more resembled a store with a backroom where the work was done.) After walking through the showroom, we were led into a dingy room with wood shavings and sawdust strewn about on a bare dirt floor. Craftsmen were busy chipping away at blocks of teak or wood unknown to me, and their tools and equipment were so crude, I could not understand how they could turn out such beautiful objects. The "vise" consisted of a stump of a tree, upright, with a wooden wedge driven into the top as one jaw of the vise, and the other jaw was a bare left or right foot. The worker's seat was a rough wooden bench or chair. His hammer consisted of a conical piece of wood, not unlike a large ice cream cone or a chalice. Three or four artisans toiled under a single bare light bulb, and all with similarly crude equipment.

Walking back into the souvenir shop was a stark contrast to the workroom. Here, the lights shone brightly, and the highly polished carvings could just as easily have been in Harrods of London! My friend and I looked at animals, bowls, chessmen, and other objects from teak wood, lemon wood, or other exotic wood. We each looked for that perfect souvenir. (But one that we could mail home!) One very large elephant at the entrance to the store was approximately five feet high, exquisitely carved from one piece of teak. We were told we could have the carving (free) if either of us could carry it away. Neither of us could even budge it, nor could we move it together! It must have weighed several hundred pounds minimum. I finally purchased a carved lemonwood basket with handle and a teakwood elderly Chinese man holding a cane. These I sent to my parents after returning to the base.

Next we visited a parasol factory where we watched an amazing transformation of plain parasols into the most exquisitely painted works of art. We saw paper being made (paper used for packing, not good quality writing paper), jewelry being crafted from pure silver, and observed many other crafts and trades. I sent home one parasol and one large silver brooch, in addition to the wood carvings.

The most interesting experience I had in Cheng Mei was riding an elephant and seeing them move teak logs. I learned that a young boy is assigned to a baby elephant and they are together for life. The boy becomes the handler of the elephant and the elephant works with no one else. Once the elephant is old enough to work, the handler controls the elephant by sitting on the elephant's head and using his feet to kick behind the elephant's ears and shouting commands.

If the elephant didn't perform what was required, the handler would then prod the elephant by poking the tip of a long thin knife into the skin of the elephant's head. (The elephant's skin is quite thick, but I could see some small blood spots.)

As each new batch of tourists arrived to watch the elephants work, the command was given and all work stopped. The tourists were told that a "food fee" must be paid in order for the elephants to eat so they could then work for the tourists. After paying the fee and getting some background information, the elephants began to work again.

Two elephants worked together to lift one log onto a stack. The elephants must work together because the teak logs are too heavy for one elephant. If one elephant dropped its end of the log, the sudden weight shift would snap off the tusk(s) of the other elephant. Two handlers and two elephants must work closely together.

After watching the elephants work, and for another fee, we were offered the opportunity to ride one of the elephants. Not everyone wanted to do this, but I couldn't wait. I gave my camera to my friend, and he snapped a picture of me on the elephant. The handler sat on the head with his feet behind the elephant's ears, but the rider sits on the elephant's shoulder blades, just behind the head. Mounting is done with the elephant lying down and when the elephant got up, the shoulder blades moved up and down so much that I feared being thrown off! It was like riding two giant pistons. I had to hold on to the handler to stay on.

Alas, after three days of fun, it was time to head back to the Air Force base. We boarded the same C–47 for our trip, and again after takeoff, the pilot seemed concerned with the left engine. One month later, we received word that the very C–47 we had flown, crashed on take–off in Viet Nam and all on board were killed. The left engine had failed during takeoff.

Dirty Pictures

People with idle time and a good imagination can think up all sorts of mischievous things to do. Add a good knowledge of electronics, and that unspent energy can be directed at some shocking tricks.

Someone in the Comm/Nav (Communications and Navigation) shop obtained an empty cardboard cigar box, then a small group of us gathered metallic tape, a battery, a transformer and a micro–switch, and set to work. Each end of the box was wrapped with the metallic tape, leaving a narrow gap around the middle of the box. The tape was then sliced along the lid so that it could be opened. The battery and transformer were placed into the box and wired through the micro switch to the tape sections. Then the micro–switch was mounted to the inside of the box so that when the lid was opened, the battery voltage was applied through the transformer to the two tape sections. The result was that if someone held the box and opened the lid; zap! The person would receive quite a shock. To entice people to fall into the trap, we labeled the box "Dirty Pictures." We all laughed as our cohorts were surprised (one by one) by the shock, but then we panicked when the captain in charge of the shop walked in unannounced. We tried to look busy. The captain walked around the shop looking at this and that, and, after chatting with a few people, finally walked over to the table and picked up the box. He frowned when he saw the label on the box and we thought he might chew us out, but then he opened the box, probably to see if it really contained what it said it did. He let out a yell, threw the box down, and retreated out the door, while mumbling something unintelligible. We didn't see him the rest of that day, or the next day. In retrospect, if we had known the results, we might have done it sooner!

Leaving Thailand

While I was in Thailand, my brother married his high school sweetheart, but I couldn't be there for the wedding since I was on the other side of the world. Greg and his new wife had moved to England (due to Greg's job), so when my tour of duty in Thailand was completed, I decided to visit them on my way home.

Since I had been sent directly to the Air Force Base, I did not have a passport, nor the required visas. Inquiring into the necessary preparations left me with a list of things to do, but I had planned ahead, so I would be ready. I also discovered the existence an "embassy flight" twice a week, which I could board for free. This flight (or series of flights) continued around the world in both directions to ferry personnel and cargo to various embassies. I submitted the necessary request for the flight to England.

First though, I needed to visit the American Embassy in Bangkok, Thailand, to get my passport. I was told that I needed no foreign country visas, as I would be on the Embassy flight.

The day finally arrived. With all my belongings in tow (one large blue "duffel bag" and a couple of carry–on bags), I arrived at the Bangkok Airport. When I got to the security people, I handed them my passport, and they kept trying to ask me questions, but I couldn't understand them. I did speak some basic Thai, but couldn't make any sense of what he was saying. Finally, someone else (who spoke English) asked, "How did you get into Thailand?" Oh yeah. I guess that would be a logical question, since I had a passport originating in Thailand! Then I remembered that I was supposed to give them a copy of a letter (my orders—simplified) to explain how I had come into the country. After that, all went smoothly—that is, until I got to the check–in for the embassy flight.

The embassy flight would pass through India (Calcutta), and for that country, I *did* need a visa! They would not allow me to board the aircraft without a visa. I panicked! Leaving my luggage with them, I hurried out of the airport and jumping into a taxi said, "hurry, I need to get to the Indian Embassy!"

I arrived at the Indian Embassy and immediately made my request with the administrative personnel. Everything at the Indian Embassy seemed to be in slow motion. I don't think they would get excited if their Sari was on fire. Anyway, I was told that it takes three days to get a visa to India. I told them I don't have three days! I was finally ushered into the Ambassador's office, and after talking to him for a short while, he agreed to allow me to get the visa immediately.

With the proper visa stamps in my passport, I again jumped in the cab and we careened through the streets of Bangkok like a mad bee on a suicide mission. I arrived back at the boarding place for the embassy flight an hour before flight time. Unfortunately, I was told the doors were closed and I could not board. I complained and poured out my story, but kept getting the same answer.

One of the "conditions" of scheduling to fly on the embassy flight was the guarantee that one would have sufficient funds in hand to get to the destination by commercial flights in case of being "bumped." (Or, apparently, if one is not allowed to get on the flight.) So, I had received an "advance" on my pay and was (thankfully) prepared.

After getting nowhere with the personnel at the embassy flight desk, I wandered over to the Swiss Air desk. Yes, they had a flight leaving soon, and yes, they could put me on it. $601.34 later (or lighter!), I walked back to the embassy flight desk and retrieved my bags. The ticket agent walked with me and actually carried my duffel bag to the Swiss Air counter and checked it in for me. I was treated like royalty!

White knuckles

From Bangkok, Thailand to London, England, the Swiss Air flight would make stops at: Calcutta, India; Karachi, Pakistan; Athens, Greece; and Zurich, Switzerland.

As we approached Calcutta, we flew directly through one of many thunderstorms in the area, and lightening seemed to be forming just off the wingtip in the clouds. The lightening began as a blue ball, and then a white flash streaked earthward. I pressed my face against the window, trying to see as much of God's fireworks show as I could. The airplane was lurching forward, up, down, and sideways, making it difficult to even look out of the small window. As I looked to my left briefly, I saw the women next to me gripping the arm rest so tightly that her knuckles were totally white. She saw me looking at her and said through clenched teeth, "How can you keep staring out the window like that? Aren't you scared?" I said, "No, I'm fascinated by the lightening." She didn't seem to appreciate my lack of concern and she maintained her hold on the armrest until we landed. *"If you make the Most High your dwelling — even the LORD, who is my refuge — then no harm will befall you, no disaster will come near your tent. For he will command his angels concerning you to guard you in all your ways; they will lift you up in their hands, so that you will not strike your foot against a stone. You will tread upon the lion and the cobra; you will trample the great lion and the serpent. 'Because he loves me,' says the LORD, 'I will rescue him; I will protect him, for he acknowledges my name. He will call upon me, and I will answer him; I will be with him in trouble, I will deliver him and honor him. With long life will I satisfy him and show him my salvation.'"* (Psalms 91:9–16)

Athens

The flight from Calcutta to Athens was uneventful. Since Athens was a short layover and refueling stop, I remained on board. Since I was still seated by the window, I was watching the land pass by beneath us, then I saw the shoreline and we were over water. But then we made a sharp turn (and a long turn), and I noticed that we were going back over the shoreline, but in the opposite direction. We were going back to Athens. I mentioned this to the new passenger in the seat to my left, and he said, "No, we're just banking. We haven't turned around." But we soon landed — at the Athens airport. After touching down and taxiing to the terminal, the pilot announced over the intercom that the landing gear could not be raised, and we would have to wait in the terminal for another airplane to be flown to Athens, to continue the flight. I decided that not getting the landing gear up was much better than not being able to get the landing gear down, but many passengers were unhappy and were giving the stewardesses a hard time. I really felt sorry for them as I thought they were doing an excellent job of being helpful, patient, and friendly.

After a four hour wait, we boarded the replacement plane, and took off. I felt compelled to write a note commending the stewardesses on their job. They were extremely patient and calm even with business men screaming at them. I found a form in the seat pocket, filled it out, and sealed it. I then gave it to one of the stewardesses, per the instructions on the form, to be turned in to Swiss Air headquarters. The stewardess looked at me with a pained expression and said, "Oh, is this a complaint?" I quickly said, "No! Quite the contrary! This is a compliment. You all did a marvelous job. I wish I had let you read it before I sealed the envelope." She looked as though she didn't quite believe me, but she obviously submitted my letter to the airline, as I later received a personal note from the President of Swiss Air, thanking me for my comments on the good performance of the airline staff.

"Do not withhold good from those to whom it is due, when it is in the power of your hand to do so." (Proverbs 3:27)

Choice Assignment

According to the "promises" made to those airmen returning from a tour of duty in Southeast Asia, our next duty assignment (geographical area in the USA) was to be *our* choice. Since there were three of us coming from the same place at the same time with the same training and experience, this should have been a shoe–in. I wanted the east coast, another wanted California, and the third wanted the Middle of the country.

I suspect someone in personnel did not enjoy their job, and attempted (at every opportunity) to make everyone else's life miserable. I was stationed next at McConnell AFB in Kansas, the California requester went to the east coast, and the Midwest requester went to California. I had already discovered not to believe all the promises we received, but after having my orders "lost" on my Thailand assignment (thereby causing my promotions to be 6 months behind everyone else and losing "leave" time), and all the other difficulties encountered, I'm not sure if God was making sure I didn't reenlist, or if this is normal activity.

LBJ

President Lyndon Johnson visited McConnell Air Force Base during my tour at the base. Almost everyone from the base came to the flight line to watch him arrive. It was very crowded, so another airman and I climbed onto the roof of a tug motor (used to tow airplanes) so that we could see. The President was heading our way, but after greeting people along his route, he turned and headed in another direction. It appeared that we would not be able to get close to him, so we went back to the radio shop. Once there, we watched the small television that someone had brought in, and saw President

Johnson walk to the tug motor that we had just been sitting on! We left too soon.

Little Authority?

It was unusual to be at work and not in uniform during my Air Force days, but sometimes a short trip to the "office" was necessary to pick up a paycheck or drop off some paperwork. One such day I was in the radio shop and everyone else was out of the room for some reason. I knew all the people who worked in my group and the two groups adjoining ours (Navigation [NAV] and Electronic Counter Measures [ECM]), so when an unknown person walked into the room and looked around, I asked, "Are you looking for someone with a little authority?" He said, "Yes." I said, "Well, I'll help you, I've got about as little authority as anyone around here." He laughed and I helped him with what he needed.

The radio shop had the responsibility for installing crystals in an AGM (Air to Ground Missile) remote control system, and these crystals were kept in a safe until we received orders to install a matched set, one in the missile and one in the aircraft. All of the ECM material was classified and therefore was kept in the same safe as the crystals. The safe was located in a walk–in wire cage that was also kept locked in the ECM group work area.

While scheduled for the evening shift, I came to the office during the day to pick up my paycheck. (Again in civilian clothes) As I waited for my boss to return to his office, one of the airmen from the ECM group (whom I knew) asked if I could open the safe for him. I was unlocking the safe inside the wire cage, dressed in civilian clothes, when a lieutenant walked up behind me and asked, "Who are you and what are you doing here?" I told him who I was and then explained that the ECM Airman had asked me to open the safe for him. The lieutenant then questioned my authority to be there, so I said, "Wouldn't you think that if your people come to me to open the safe for them, and I have the combination for the safe, that I might have the authority to open it?" He couldn't argue with logic and allowed me to continue. I guess he wouldn't have done his job if he hadn't questioned me.

Jet Exhaust

Anyone who has spent a winter in Kansas (or any of "the plains states") will know what I mean when I say the winters can be VERY cold and windy. On one such wintry day, I was working on an F–105 aircraft on the flight line. The wiring access hatch on the bottom of the aircraft is only big enough for a skinny person (which I was, weighing only 140 pounds at the time) to enter wearing only the essentials (fatigues). I had to remove my parka and gloves. I then had to enter the hatch with my arms straight up and work over my head. It was impossible to raise or lower one's arms inside the compartment. It was definitely not a place for anyone with claustrophobia.

Once in the wiring compartment, I worked quickly but after only a short while I had to slip out and put on my parka and gloves to warm up for another go. Even with the heavy winter gear, warming up was next to impossible.

Nearby, an F–105 was warming up for takeoff. The jet's engine was idling, and because I was a safe distance from the running jet, I moved directly into the path of the exhaust. Ahhh... warmth! I was just getting comfortable when the pilot increased the throttle to pull the jet out of its parking space and down the ramp to the runway. The cement ramp (flight line) was spotted with large patches of ice and as the strong blast of jet exhaust hit me, it knocked me over backwards and sent me sliding along on the ice. I wasn't hurt; in fact I was laughing as I slid (and hoping no one was watching).

Blackbird

The radio shop personnel constantly monitored the tower frequency to determine when flights were taking off and landing. All the shops had to be available just prior to and during takeoff and immediately after landing. But once the airplanes were all on the ground and no radio trouble had been reported, we usually allowed all but two people to leave for the rest of the shift.

In late 1967 or early 1968, with two of us "manning the fort" a call came over the tower frequency requesting "special" permission to land, and saying his HF (High Frequency) radio was not working. Because the call sign was strange and the pilot requested permission to forego the standard landing procedures, our interest was aroused! We both high tailed it to the flight line to see what sort of airplane this was.

A solid cloud cover kept us from seeing the sky that day, but even so, we should have seen the aircraft approaching the downwind end of the runway by now. Suddenly we saw the strangest aircraft we had ever seen—not approaching from downwind, but dropping straight down out of the clouds over the middle of the runway! From a vertical drop the airplane flared out, rolled a short way down the runway, turned up the ramp and into an open hanger doorway. The doors of the hanger closed immediately and an Air Police truck came to a screeching halt just outside the hangar. Air Policemen spilled out of the truck, surrounding the hanger and standing guard with M–16 rifles at the ready.

My coworker and I looked at each other with our mouths hanging open and without a word we raced back to the radio shop. We were the only aircraft radio shop on base, so it stood to reason that we would find out about this aircraft when they called us to come fix the radio. We sat waiting for the call, but it never came.

On the following day, a C–135 cargo aircraft arrived with a full complement of maintenance crew and equipment for the "bird" in the hanger. I was very disappointed that we were not going to find out more about the aircraft or see it up close.

A few days later, we again heard that strange call sign on the tower frequency. This time the pilot asked for clearance to take off. The whole radio shop (and others, after we excitedly spread the word) ran to the flight line to watch the aircraft take off. The hangar doors opened and the aircraft pulled out, turned down the ramp and onto the middle of the runway. While completing the turn onto the runway, the pilot gave full throttle and sped down the runway. After traveling only one quarter of the runway length, the aircraft lifted off and immediately shot vertically, like a rocket, into the clouds. I never saw an aircraft perform like this, especially one this large.

Almost 30 years later, I again saw the mysterious aircraft (when it was declassified), and learned that the strange aircraft that I had seen was the SR–71 "Blackbird." It is still an amazing airplane.

High C

Joe and I were roommates while stationed in Kansas. We took a 3 day weekend off and I accompanied him to his home in St. Louis, where I met his family, his fiancée, and several of his friends. One evening, Joe, his fiancée, and I went to a very popular (and exclusive) restaurant. Joe ordered a carafe of wine while we waited for our food to arrive. During the conversation I kept rubbing my finger around the rim of the glass, causing it to make a "singing" sound (one note of course). The sound was very loud and piercing, but of such a pitch that no one could tell where it was coming from. All conversation in the restaurant quieted and then stopped. Before the room got totally quiet and before anyone could figure out where the high pitched tone was coming from, I stopped rubbing the glass. When the conversation again rose to a good level, I again began rubbing my finger around the glass, producing that irritating sound. The conversations quickly died down so I again ceased rubbing the glass. At this point Joe leaned over and quietly said, "I don't think you should do that again—they *will* throw us out." I heeded Joe's advice, and we enjoyed our meal before leaving peaceably.

George AFB

During my assignment in Kansas, I was sent "TDY" (Temporary Duty) a few times to George AFB in California. McConnell AFB in Kansas was a pilot training base (for F–105 fighter/Bombers), and George AFB was the gunnery and bombing training base. Our job while at George AFB was to provide maintenance for the squadron during training flights.

During one of my short stays at George AFB, a film crew and entertainers arrived to film a troop entertainment show similar to Bob Hope's USO shows. This show was called "Operation Entertainment." Whenever we had a break, our group wandered the short distance from our temporary shop in one of the hangers to the part of the ramp where the stage had been erected. We enjoyed watching the show. Tim Conway, Gloria Loring, Florence Henderson and a few other celebrities were on hand as well as a live band. Some of the band members looked familiar, but I didn't know their names then and certainly wouldn't remember them now anyway.

After the first day of filming, the entertainers, band members and crew piled onto a bus and were driven away. My coworkers and I finished our duty, ate supper in the chow hall, and then someone suggested that we go to a place I had not heard of before, "Roy Rogers' Apple Valley Inn." One member of our group had access to a car, so after changing into civilian clothes we drove to the Inn to see what it was like.

The lounge at the Inn was no different than any other lounge—dim, smoky, and noisy. When we arrived, the place was already packed and we found only one table with a couple of chairs, right by an upright piano across the room from the bar. My coworkers sat at the table and I sat on the piano bench next to them. Since the piano was not presently in use, this was an adequate, if not very comfortable, solution.

After we had been there a short while, I looked up to see Tim Conway, Florence Henderson, and a few others from the "Operation Entertainment" show approaching the piano. One of the band members accompanying them asked me if he could play the piano. I said, "Sure," as I got up to give him the piano bench. He said, "No, stay seated... I only need half of it." So there I sat on half of a piano bench with this man banging out music, and Tim Conway, Florence Henderson, and other celebrities on the other side of the piano, singing their hearts out. (And laughing, joking, etc.) That day I learned that Tim Conway was just as funny off camera as he was on camera. This was an evening I would never forget.

The next day the "Operation Entertainment" crew and cast were back at work. During a break in the filming we got a chance to chat with them. After reminding them that we saw them the night before (I'm sure they remembered the skinny kid on the piano bench), I talked Tim Conway into getting his photo taken with me while he wore my cap. He was agreeable and that photo is one of my favorites! (I never thought to get an autograph!) At the end of the work day (theirs and ours), we said goodbye to the celebrities and crew and waved as the bus took them away. The filming was finished so we didn't see them again.

The cap I usually wore (not the one Tim Conway had worn in the photo), was a Khaki baseball type cap. As a symbol of the radio shop and electronics in general, I had fastened a resistor (vertically) to the front of the cap, just above the visor. The resistor was not a glaring addition, but I was always surprised that I got away with having an adornment of that sort.

Although I was never confronted about the resistor on the cap, I was challenged about the cap itself while at George AFB. I was walking back to the flight area (our hanger) from the chow hall when two Air Policemen approached from the opposite direction. They stopped me and said the base commander did not allow baseball style caps to be worn on the base. I said, "Ok," and took the cap off. Then the same airman said, "But you have to wear a hat." So, I put the cap back on. Then he said, "But you can't wear *that* cap." I think I took the cap off and put it on two or three times, each time simply saying, "Ok." When I realized this might go on for a while, I informed both of them that I was there on temporary duty, and the cap I wore was the only one I had brought with me. They finally saw the futility of the situation and allowed me to proceed on my way. I enjoyed a good chuckle over the situation.

Green Cloud

After an honorable discharge from the USAF, I accepted a job at a local electric control panel fabrication company. I began working in the shop, hand drilling holes in small panels for the installation of switches and other electrical components. One day as I diligently performed my job after a night out that included draft beer, I released a particularly pungent green cloud no more than two seconds before my boss appeared out of nowhere and bent down right behind me to pick something up from the floor. I noticed he didn't spend much time in that position, so he either very quickly found what he needed, or decided it was not a good time to retrieve what he was looking for.

At the end of two weeks, the personnel manager asked me to work in the drafting department, which meant better pay and cleaner work (and "elevator music", if you could call that a benefit). Because I liked drawing better than drilling and had some experience, I agreed. The shop foreman said he was sorry to see me go as he had finally found someone capable of drilling a straight hole with a hand drill. I guess he forgave me for the unintentional green cloud.

Fire in the Microwave

The company I worked for built and wired control panels from the smallest size to large walk–in units. These control panels might be used in power plants, grain elevators, or other large electrical equipment locations. Not everyone in the company, however, was knowledgeable about wiring and electric circuits. In the drafting department, for instance, the engineers designed the circuits and then gave rough drawings to the draftsmen to create the finished diagrams. One young man was hired because of his acquaintance with one of the engineers, but he knew nothing about electricity. Once, in the break room, the young man put a paper lunch bag containing loose popcorn into the microwave to pop it. When he pressed "start," the top of the bag immediately burst into flames and we heard a loud "snap, crack and pop." He quickly hit the stop button and pulled the bag out, blowing the flames out. When he asked me why that happened, I explained that he had made a "tank circuit" by wrapping the top of the bag with a wire "twisty." The wire (tank circuit) heated up when the microwave tube began radiating, causing the paper bag to catch on fire. He didn't believe me and sought out his engineer friend to get the correct answer. The engineer said, "You made a tank circuit by wrapping the wire–tie around the top of the bag, and it heated up when you put it into the microwave oven." Imagine that.

Ham Salad

During my one year of employment in this company, as well as the following year when I attended a technical school in Harrisburg, Pennsylvania, Mom packed a lunch for me every day. This lunch consisted of a ham–salad sandwich, a thermos of tomato soup, a couple of cookies, perhaps some chips or other "munchies," and a second thermos of milk. (Everyone told me that my lunchbox was bigger inside than outside.) Mom kept asking me if I would rather have something else for lunch, as she was afraid I would grow tired of eating the same thing day after day. I told her that I really liked the lunch menu and was never tired of it. I suspect she got tired of preparing the same thing every day. Only when I moved to Maryland to begin a career with a large communications corporation did I end the lunch menu that I loved so much. Of course Mom was no longer close enough to make my ham salad and tomato soup lunch each day.

Fly

After one year as a draftsman I received a raise of ten cents per hour and realized this was not a good job for a career. I decided to go back to school. I heard about Electronic Institutes (EI) through a friend who had attended, and so I decided to attend. The Harrisburg branch of EI was located in an old store built along the Susquehanna River. Once into the building, large wooden doors with transoms (a window above the door that could be tilted open) led to classrooms on the left and right. Straight ahead was the office area. The transoms were usually left open to allow air to flow from one room to another, while the doors were closed during class time.

One warm day while working on a project, the student next to me caught a large fly. Another student pulled a loose thread from his shirt and I printed a very small sign that read "HELP!" I tied the sign to one end of the thread and the other end of the thread to one of the fly's legs. We then released the fly and watched to see where it would go. The fly rose ever so slowly. It looked like one of those small airplanes with a banner following behind as it headed straight through the transom. We assumed, with disappointment, this would be the end of the story and we would never know what happened to the fly.

After a short while, engrossed in our work and forgetting all about the fly, the classroom door opened and the dean of the school entered. While it was unusual to see him in the classroom, we didn't think much about why he was there. As soon as all eyes were on him, he said, "OK, who's the wise guy sending help messages tied onto a fly?" The whole class laughed, but not as hard as the three of us who knew what he meant! He went on to explain that while he was sitting at his desk working, a large fly with a help sign tied to one leg landed in front of him. We confessed. Fortunately, the only consequence of our prank was lots more laughter.

Tubes

EI was a technical school devoted to teaching Electronic Theory and practical application. An EI graduate's goal was to procure a job in the electronics industry, typically in the communications field.

Lessons progressed from very basic electricity to complicated electronic circuits, both digital and analog. By this time, most of the industry had transitioned from tubes to transistors and integrated circuits, but many older pieces of equipment were still in use, therefore the industry (and also the school) still required knowledge of tube theory. During "vacuum tube theory" class one day, the instructor was giving the history and reasoning behind the development of the pentode (a 5–element tube). "The first tube was simply a gate," he said, "having a cathode and anode (plate). (A diode vacuum tube) It either allowed the flow of current, or blocked it. Hence, a grid was added between the two elements, called a 'control grid.' It was so called because it controlled the amount of current flow, and now you could have no flow, full flow, or any amount in between. (A triode vacuum tube) However, when the flow was minimal, the spacing of the elements inside the tube caused the flow of electrons to be erratic or stop abruptly. There was not enough attraction by the plate (positive charge) to move the electrons reliably across the void. A 'screen grid' was then added between the control grid and the plate to help accelerate the electrons from the cathode to the plate. This sometimes sped up the electrons too much, and caused the 'kadink effect.'" At this point, I began chuckling, because I sensed what was coming next.

The instructor paused after introducing the kadink effect and sure enough, one of the students asked, "What is the kadink effect?" The instructor said, "That's where the electrons are going so fast that they careen off the plate, and hit the glass, going kadink, kadink, kadink." I was laughing really hard now, while most of the students were busily taking notes. Then the instructor added, "So the final grid is the 'suppressor grid' and that was added to slow the electrons enough so that they wouldn't hit the glass." By now, I think all the students were wise to the joke. Thank goodness for my prior tube knowledge. I might have been busy scribbling notes as well.

Chapter III: The beginning of signs

Marriage

"But as it is written: 'Eye has not seen, nor ear heard, nor have entered into the heart of man the things which God has prepared for those who love Him.'" (1Corinthians 2:9) Many have been the signs and wonders in my life, but none so wonderful as my meeting, marriage, and life with Alice.

At the completion of tech school (finishing number two in my class), I accepted a job with a major communications company, and moved to Maryland. That's where we pick up the next story—about two years into my career.

Before I met Alice, I dated a girl introduced to me by a coworker. She lived in a first floor garden apartment of a high–rise building. Instead of going through the lobby, where I would have to be buzzed in, then wait while the receptionist called ahead to make sure I was allowed to visit, I simply knocked on her patio door and she would let me in. One day I arrived before she had gotten home. After knocking and getting no response, I returned to my car and saw June, the girl my roommate, Tim, dated. (They had been introduced by my girlfriend)

June invited me to wait in her apartment, on the seventh floor, directly above my girlfriend's apartment. It was while I was waiting in June's apartment sipping on a drink that I met June's roommate, Alice. Alice arrived home and sat on the far side of the small living room. June, Alice and I were talking but pretty soon the conversation was mostly between Alice and me. The more we talked, the more interested in her I became. While I didn't actually see sparks flying, I'm sure they were there.

After a while we were interrupted by a knock at the door, which turned out to be my girlfriend looking for me. She had an idea where to look for me when she saw my car in the parking lot. She must have sensed the sparks flying between Alice and me because after she sat down next to me, she kept nudging closer and closer until she was practically sitting on my lap. Although she kept suggesting that we leave, I was in no hurry to go.

I called Alice a few times and sparks still flew, even over the phone lines. We agreed to spend a day together on Tim's cabin cruiser on the Chesapeake Bay. Tim, June, Alice and I had a wonderful time on the boat that day. I was hooked. I've heard that when you meet the right one, you will know. I knew. I have no doubts even after 35 years! The girl I was dating when I met Alice knew that it was over between us and said (sarcastically), "I hope you two are very happy together!" I know she really didn't mean it, but I accepted the blessing! Very conveniently, my (now EX) girlfriend moved away.

Tim and I had been renting a house, and Alice and June rented a two–bedroom apartment. The four of us spent some time together, but more often June came to the house to see Tim, and I went to the apartment to see Alice. One day when Alice and I were in her apartment and June and Tim were out somewhere, I proposed to Alice and she accepted. Tim and June walked in a little while later and said, "We have some news for you. We're getting married!" I looked at Alice, and we began laughing, and said, "We are too!"

I firmly believe God arranged our lives. Only He could orchestrate the way we met, the way we knew we were meant for each other, and the crazy way things worked out for the four of us. I still look back and smile as I think how God worked everything out. We were simply changing roommates! But read on! There's more!

With wedding plans in the works, planning for the future took a whole different turn (actually, I had no future plans before this). Tim and June wanted to continue renting, and Alice and I wanted to buy a house. So, June moved into the rented house that Tim and I shared, while I moved into the apartment with Alice and we began searching for a house. Everything worked out perfectly! God deals quite well with details. But I'm getting ahead of myself! First, there was the wedding!

Alice and I were married in July, at Alice's parents' farm in Illinois. With only our families present, it was a very small wedding. The ceremony was planned for the front lawn, which seemed like a safe choice for the normally dry month of July. However, in this particular year, July was a very rainy month. Rain fell steadily for two weeks before our wedding day, flooding fields and lawns alike. The day before the wedding, I had waded into the garden knee–deep in water and ankle–deep in mud, to find some cucumbers for lunch. The odor from the stagnant water was not very pleasant either.

God was at work, however. Just as He caused dry land to appear for the Israelites to pass through the Red Sea, the rain stopped that evening, the wind changed direction, and by morning the front lawn was dry enough to support folding chairs! Clouds were nowhere to be seen and the sun shone brightly for a perfect wedding day! Even the smell was gone due to the changed wind direction.

Following the ceremony we went to Alice's aunt's house for the reception, again on the front lawn. Alice and I then drove to St. Louis to visit my Air Force roommate Joe, and his wife. Approximately three o'clock that afternoon, it began raining again, and continued through the next week.

Alice and I agreed that God's planning is perfect, and the sign shown to us on our wedding day confirms that God cares about every detail of our lives.

Gateway to the West

While in St. Louis, Alice and I visited the "Arch". The trip to the top is a great experience, but it's not for the claustrophobic! The view from the top (on a clear day) is well worth the trip. Although Alice and I spent only one day in St. Louis, the memory of the visit to the arch stayed with us.

In 1980, Alice and I traveled to New Mexico to attend a custody hearing for her two nieces, Ada and Carey, and then bring them back with us to Maryland. We had received a plea from their mother

(Alice's sister–in–law) several months before, asking if we would take the girls in, if anything happened to her. Of course we agreed, not thinking that anything was going to happen to her, but then she got cancer and died within weeks of the diagnosis. Alice's brother and sister–in–law had divorced and the sister–in–law had remarried, but her new husband already had a six year old mentally challenged son, and couldn't handle two very active girls (ages 9 and 13) as well. So we found ourselves driving to New Mexico and then back to Maryland. Our own two children were left in the care of my brother and sister–in–law until we returned home.

While traveling from New Mexico to Maryland, pulling a large U–Haul trailer and Alice's two nieces in the car with us, we found ourselves in St. Louis and nearing the Arch. Alice suggested that we stop and allow Ada and Carey to see the Arch, as they might enjoy it and it would give me a break from driving. So we visited the arch and rode the cramped little cars to the top. After reaching the top and while peering out through the small windows, I realized it had been seven years *to the day* since our first trip up the arch. We were actually spending our seventh anniversary in the very spot that we visited on our wedding day. There are no coincidences, only God–incidents! Seven is God's number of perfection (God created the world and all that is in it in six days, and rested on the seventh day), and although I still do not understand the significance of the occasion, I truly know that God orchestrated another amazing God–incident. Perhaps He was just letting us know that He is still in charge. We were so busy with the details and work involved in getting Ada and Carey moved, we never thought about what day it was. *I* didn't think about it anyway, and if Alice thought about it, she wasn't saying anything.

Gas TV

Shortly after Alice and I were married, she invited me to a party of fellow teachers from her school. Because Alice was the only person I knew, I tried to find a quiet, out–of–the–way place to relax. I found a small group sitting in one corner of the living room, quietly talking, so I joined them. The conversation turned to childhood remembrances, like when their family had gotten their first TV, telephone, or other "new" technology. One person shared that they were the first house to have a telephone in their neighborhood and all the neighbors came over to use it. Another person talked about their first TV and how they were the envy of the neighborhood. I sat there quietly, just listening. After each of the other members of our small group had spoken, there was a lull in the conversation. I chose this moment to speak. I began slowly and very seriously, as though reflecting on my past, "I remember when we got our first TV, but since we didn't have electricity, we got a gas TV." Dead silence. Slowly, after a second or two, the laughter began and steadily rose. The roar from our small group got so loud that all the other groups stopped talking to find out what we were laughing at. This was one of my greatest moments of ad–libbing.

Many years later I submitted the gas TV story to a company publication and they printed it. I was surprised when a technician in another state called to ask, "How did that work? We had a gas refrigerator, but I can't figure out how a gas TV would work." P. T. Barnum once said, "There's a sucker born every minute." I guess he was right.

Long Wait?

One of the benefits of living in Montgomery County, Maryland, is the Olney Ale House. This is an old "Inn" style house that always reminds me of a 1700's roadhouse. I always feel as though I'm in a slower, more relaxed time. The waiting area, which is extremely small, is situated just inside the entrance, next to the barroom seating area and the bar itself. Just past this area is a doorway to the front room seating area, and that room looks out onto Route 108 and the Olney Theater across the road. Many people come to the Ale House before going to the theater, so the clientele varies from extremely casual (motorcycle riders) to the extremely well–dressed theater–goers.

For many years this restaurant has been the best place to get homemade food, including their famous oatmeal molasses bread and chunky beef stew. Not to mention the large variety of beer and ale available.

One evening years ago, our family chose to go to the Ale House for supper. Normally, we arrived early to avoid the crowds, but we arrived to find it already crowded. The small waiting area was packed. The wait was to be thirty to forty–five minutes according to the young lady seating people. I gave the hostess my name and we stood just inside the door, waiting for a spot on one of the two benches to open up so we could sit while we waited. Pretty soon, Alice and I could sit down, but our children had to remain standing. After another ten minutes, I heard the hostess call, "Moses!" I immediately said out loud, "*HOW* long is the wait?" Everyone laughed except one older woman who gave me icy glances as she followed the hostess to her seat.

Flour

Alice's mom and dad visited us every March for the national square dance at Sheraton Park in Washington, D.C. This worked out well as it was also the time of our son's birthday. During one visit, Alice's mom, Alice, and I were sitting in the kitchen talking and the conversation turned to cooking (as it ALWAYS does when Alice and her mother are together). Conversions when measuring quantities are often confusing. Alice looked at her mom very seriously and asked, "How many cups of sugar are in a five pound bag of flour?" Alice's mom looked at her, and then looked at me, and I at her, then we both looked at Alice. Thinking her mom hadn't heard her, she repeated the question: "How many cups of sugar are in a five pound bag of flour?" We again all looked at each other, and I said, "Is this a trick question?" Alice still didn't realized what she had said, but after making her aware of it, we all laughed until it hurt and tears rolled down Alice's cheeks from laughing.

Masked Intruder

Alice and I were sound asleep. It was around midnight and the next day was a work day. Suddenly we were awakened by what sounded like heavy footsteps in the hallway just outside our bedroom door. Thump, thump, thump. With my heart in my throat and pounding so hard I could hear it, I jumped out of bed, found my .22 caliber revolver in the night stand and began loading it. As soon as the gun was loaded, I dialed 911, all the while watching the bedroom door, expecting it to fly open at any moment. The police were there within 2 minutes! (The fastest response I've ever known.) I handed the phone to Alice, and crept to the door as quietly as I could. The dispatcher told Alice to tell me to put the gun down and open the front door for the officer. Of course I had to open the bedroom door first, so I really didn't want to put the gun down. I held onto the gun long enough to open the bedroom door and make sure there wasn't anyone in the hallway first, then I put the gun on the floor next to the bed and cautiously made my way to the front door, looking into our son's and daughter's bedrooms and the bathroom as I passed by them. Finally, I opened the front door, but saw no one, so I stuck my head out and looked to the right to find the officer pressed against the front of the house looking at me. That officer followed me into the house and was soon joined by a second officer. I explained what I had heard, and the three of us searched the whole house, even looking into the attic. I also climbed onto the roof, but found neither a person, nor any sign of entry.

After a thorough search, the officers departed and Alice and I went back to bed. Neither of us could sleep so we just laid there with our eyes closed. Soon we again heard thump, thump, thump, I grabbed my gun along with a flashlight and carefully opened the bedroom door. No sign of anyone in the hallway. I tiptoed to the dining room, living room, and kitchen, but saw nothing out of the ordinary. As I neared the bedroom again, I realized the sound was coming from overhead! Something was either in the attic or on the roof! Access to the attic was by way of a pull–down folding stairs in the hallway. I slowly pulled the trap door down while shining my flashlight into the opening. After the stairs were fully extended, I slowly climbed up so that I could ever–so–slowly raise my head through the opening. With the gun in one hand and the flashlight in the other, I scanned the attic. In the area over our bedroom, I saw two beady eyes staring at me through a black mask. It was a raccoon! The "footsteps" I had heard was the raccoon jumping over the ceiling joist. The raccoon had pulled the insulation aside and was building a nest.

Alice and I finally got a little sleep that night. The following day I looked around the outside of the house and discovered where the raccoon had climbed up the downspout, sat in the crook of the downspout (where it connects to the guttering), and reached out far enough to push in the vent screen in the soffit to gain entrance to the attic.

I don't like loose ends and I thought the police might like to have a "conclusion" to the report of the previous night. I called the non–emergency number for the police and spoke to a female officer. I gave her the information about the original report and the approximate time. When she had the information in front of her, I told her the rest of the story. She burst into laughter and I said, "Its funny now, but it sure wasn't funny last night."

The raccoon left and as far as I know, never came back. I repaired the vent opening with much heavier wire mesh. I was left wondering though; how did the raccoon know to shinny up the down spout and push in the vent screen? Masked critters are pretty smart!

Plays

Our son was around three years old, and our daughter was only one or two years old, when our family became involved in a local theater group. The theater group typically performed three plays a year: one children's play to benefit the local PTSA (Parent Teacher Student Association) and two adult plays. I was the group's videographer, recording all three plays for about six years. A few times during this period, I joined the cast, co–starring in one children's play and playing minor parts in others.

The most enjoyable adult play I acted in was: "You Can't Take it With You." In one scene, I was supposed to come in wearing a ladies' night gown and carrying an accordion. (You'll just have to see the play.) Unfortunately, the accordion wasn't to be found during one performance, and I had to go on stage without it. I doubt the audience noticed, but the director did and she let me know it after the performance. I checked up on the props person after that.

Another performance of the same play led to an even more embarrassing moment. I was supposed to enter just before the line, "What do you think, Donald," then respond with my line. I got busy backstage and didn't hear my cue, but my ears perked up when I heard, "What do you think, Donald?" I had no way of getting on stage in time and after a reasonable pause I heard, "I guess he doesn't really care." Without skipping a beat, the lines went on in my absence. That's quick thinking and great ad–libbing!

After the last performance of "You Can't Take it With You," I decided to shave off my beard of several years. I borrowed a pair of scissors and an electric razor, and headed for the dressing room. I couldn't find a trash can, so I trimmed most of the beard into a small cardboard box that I found. I then closed the box, intending to take it with me when I left and throw it away later. Not finding a mirror, I used the razor and just kept feeling where I was cutting, until I was satisfied that it was good enough.

Everyone was anxious to leave for the cast party after the final performance, and I hurriedly left the building as well. No one noticed for quite a while that I had shaved off my beard, but close to the end of the party, the word spread and people were commenting on my youthful face. One of the cast members came up to me and said, "I was looking through the dressing room after everyone had gone, just to be sure nothing was left behind, and I saw this cardboard box. When I opened it, I threw it down because there was something dark and fuzzy in it!" We all howled with laughter, because they now knew what was in the box that I had forgotten to take with me!

Supervisory laughs

Pens

Someone once said, "It's hard to soar with eagles when you work with a bunch of turkeys." Work can be a source of frustration, that's for sure. But work can also be a great source of laughs and humorous situations.

The next three stories involve my one–time supervisor, Clem. Clem was a short, thin, young man in his first assignment as a management employee. In fact, he was promoted after I arrived at the office, so for a short time we worked side–by–side as technicians. He was a likable fellow, and much of what he suffered at the hands of his tormenters was unfortunate, but then he seemed to have a knack for setting himself up as well.

I guess I would have been called a nerd by some, as I always carried felt–tip pens and a small screwdriver in my shirt pocket, usually in one of those plastic pocket protectors. There is nothing like a felt–tip pen for making nice–looking diagrams and taking notes. Clem also liked to create flow charts and diagrams for the office, but rather than getting his own pens, he borrowed mine. Invariably he would begin drawing, but then abruptly walk away on some mission, leaving the pens uncapped and lying on his desk. On the rare occasion that the pens were returned, they were completely dried up. This routine happened several times, but the end to my dilemma turned out to be rather amusing. The last time Clem borrowed my pens, I discovered he had gone to lunch and left my new pens lying on his desk with their tops removed. In his absence, I applied contact cement to the pens and caps, recapped the pens, and left for lunch myself.

When I returned, I walked past Clem's desk but he was not there and I saw no pens either. I thought I might never find out what had happened to them, until I glanced into the waste basket next to his desk. There were all of my pens with their tops nearly chewed off. I guess teeth make a good vise, as long as you have good teeth. He never said a word to me about the experience, but he never borrowed my pens again either.

Peanuts

Many private corporations during the 1970's and 80's cut back on personnel to save money. Our communications company was no exception. After several people left the office and were not replaced, employees began to feel the full effect of fewer numbers. My one job became multiple jobs. I became the "Equipment Installation

Coordinator," (tracking and testing the installation of equipment by the manufacturer), "Microwave Radio Repairman," "Message Test–board Technician" (the test–board was like an operator's console, used for testing long distance telephone circuits), "High Frequency and Voice Frequency Carrier Test Man," and "Supply & Inventory Person." One day, upon returning from lunch, I noticed a sealed, cardboard box on my "Equipment Installation Coordinator's" desk (I had three desks and half the office to cover), that appeared to be a delivery for my "Supply and Inventory" job and therefore should have been put into the storeroom. I was somewhat perturbed that someone had put it there, so I decided to take care of some message test–board tickets before looking at the package. While I was working on a trouble ticket, Clem returned from lunch and asked me about the box. Before I could answer, he lifted the box and a waterfall of Styrofoam "peanuts" began spilling out of the bottom. He tried to shove the box back onto the desk to stem the flow, but it was too late. Now he had a pile of "peanuts" under the box, and there was no place to set it down. The look on his face was too much for me. I burst out laughing because I realized someone had set me up, but Clem got tricked instead.

A–Frame ladder

Many things occurred in the workplace that if observed, would draw the bosses' ire. Other employees seemed to get by with unorthodox behavior, but I always got caught. One day I walked down a narrow aisle, only to find an "A–frame" ladder partially blocking my path. (An A–frame ladder is a step ladder with steps on both sides) Normally, I would just squeeze by, but this time I decided to go the direct route, so I went up one side of the ladder and down the other. What I didn't know was that Clem was directly behind me, so when I swung my leg over the top of the ladder, I almost kicked him in the head. He said, "Why did you climb over the ladder?" I said, "Because it was there!" When he just looked at me, I said, "I've always been crazy, but it keeps me from going insane." He just looked at the floor and shook his head from side to side while continuing on his way. Clem always reminded me of "snoopy," Charlie Brown's dog.

PB&J

Larry (another company supervisor) always carried a peanut butter and jelly sandwich in his sports coat pocket. As he walked around the office, he would remove it, unwrap it partially, take a bite then rewrap it and put it back into his pocket. Because Larry was known for strange behavior and sayings, one technician said "Larry is living proof that peanut butter and jelly causes brain damage."

Larry's strangeness did have a bright side. He certainly had a unique way of looking at stressful situations. On one occasion, I thought his observation of the situation was most clever, and I gained a new fondness for the man.

The office was in turmoil over a new time–accounting system. Each technician was expected to track his time by job or duty. The system was implemented without any training, so we had more questions than answers. We received no help or direction from the creators of the system. One day while expressing our frustration at the lack of instructions, Larry said, "If there are no instructions, you can't do it wrong." From that moment on we stopped worrying about the new system and spent our time doing the job we were supposed to do. Let's see... where did I put that PB&J?

That space is taken

Larry (of PB&J fame) had a cast on his right foot, due to surgery, and required a crutch to get around. One morning as he entered the parking garage, another supervisor saw him arriving and waited for him to park so he could carry Larry's briefcase for him. Larry drove one of those large station wagons from the 70's, and as he wound his way around the first floor and up the ramp to the top floor of the two story parking garage, his car went faster and faster until he was going so fast when he turned into an empty space, he hit the curb and parking meter with enough force to propel his car over the narrow median and on top of the car across from his space. You can only imagine what happens to a sub–compact car when a full–size American station–wagon drops on top of it! The other supervisor calmly walked over to Larry's car, looked up at the now double–parked vehicle and said, "Larry, you can't park there. That space is taken." I often wondered what the owner of the flattened vehicle thought when he looked for his car after work. Talk about having a bad day!

Capitol Institute of Technology

Having thoughts of higher education, I applied to Capitol Institute of Technology (CIT) seeking a two–year degree. Alice accompanied me to CIT to submit the enrollment paperwork. The secretary, who was "of a mature age," told us to wait while she informed the dean that we had arrived. She soon returned to the waiting room and said we could go into the dean's office.

Alice and I walked in and sat across the desk from the dean. After introductions the dean chuckled and said that his secretary had told him I was here with my mother. We laughed (maybe Alice wasn't laughing too much), and then in defense of his secretary the dean said to me, "you do have a very youthful face." I replied, "Did you say youthful or useful?" He laughed again, even louder.

Unfortunately, the school failed to meet my expectations (and live up to their promises), so I quit after one semester.

Elevator

The communications building I worked in housed mostly equipment, but operators and directory assistance people also worked in the building. My office was on the fourth floor along with the operators during the first few years, then more floors were added to the building and the operators were moved to a higher floor. We called our workplace an office, but more accurately it was a huge equipment room. The majority of the floor space was covered by rows of equipment, in bays from floor to ceiling.

On my way to work one morning I entered the elevator on the first floor, to find that an older woman and a young woman carrying a baby had entered the elevator ahead of me. I pressed the button for the fourth floor and noticed that the fifth floor button had already been pressed. As the doors closed and the elevator began moving, the older woman behind me said, "My, isn't he cute!" I turned around and said, "Why, thank you!" They began laughing, and after I exited on the fourth floor and the elevator doors closed, I still heard the laughter as the elevator continued up to the next floor.

Mark and Space

In the days of Morse code and then Teletype code, the "characters" (letters, numbers, and punctuation) were composed of combinations of sound (signal) and no sound (no signal), known as Mark and Space respectively.

Department stores are a great source of comic situations and comments, but you have to abandon that little voice of reason that says, "This is probably not a good idea." One such occasion happened when a young man called for his friend Mark. When his friend didn't respond, he repeated a few times: "Mark... Mark... MARK...." Getting louder each time he called. When he paused to listen for an answer each time, I interjected "space." So on it went a few times, "Mark?" "Space." "Mark?" "Space." "MARK?" "Space."

Now to the uninformed, this might not make sense, and I didn't realize at the time (due to not listening to that little voice in my head), that this might not make sense to the one calling for Mark as well. As the young man came around the corner of one isle, he caught me responding to him. Fortunately, he laughed when he realized what I was saying, and I assumed that he DID know what it meant. At least he didn't respond negatively.

Ideas always sound better until you have to explain them to someone (like running naked or eating forbidden fruit).

Phone Pickle

My first supervisor in the communication company often said, "Idle hands are the devil's workshop." It is very often true, but we got into trouble when we were busy as well. Gus, a fellow worker, decided to pull a prank on Dan, another coworker, and placed a pickle slice into the handset of Dan's phone. Gus assumed Dan would notice the pickle smell right away, open the handset and discover the source.

Not only did Dan not notice, but in time everyone forgot about it, including Gus. A few weeks later, Dan's phone became noisy and intermittent. When he took the phone apart to see what was wrong, he found the handset completely filled with a fuzzy, white mass, from the mouthpiece to the earpiece, and the wires were corroded so badly they were almost gone! The power of pickle juice!

Dangling Carrot

Reverse psychology must work, because I've seen it in action. Dan, who had received the pickle in the telephone handset, wanted a promotion. He was an excellent worker, nice guy, and really deserved to be promoted. Management at this location did not want to lose an excellent worker, however, so they would not submit his name for promotion. He then decided to do nothing, or at least very little. He slowed down to a near stand–still, which put him at risk for many more pranks by his coworkers. Gus (the same coworker who devised the pickle–in–the–phone prank) came to me with a carrot and said he wanted to hang the carrot over Dan's desk while he was out to lunch, but didn't know what to use to poke a hole through the carrot. I had a "pick set" in my hand (a head set with test probes on the end of the wires), so I held up one of the probes and said, "With a carrot hole poker of course!" That struck Gus as extremely funny and he laughed so hard, tears began rolling down his cheeks.

The carrot got hung over Dan's desk, and yes, he did get promoted. Management must have figured they weren't getting any work out of him sitting there, so they might as well let him go. Hmmm, what's the lesson here? Work hard and get nothing. Work very little and get promoted!

Union Dues

Brad was a technician who was highly excitable and unpredictable. He was a natural hippie, complete with long hair and different ideas. His political and social ideas were definitely anti–establishment, and his idea of a good financial plan was to spend money as fast as he received it, because, due to inflation it would never be worth more than it was at that moment. He hated banks and believed the safest place for money was under his mattress.

One day a group of us sat in the break–room lamenting about how much we paid in union dues when the union did nothing to help us financially while out on strike. Brad excitedly yelled, "What do we pay union doors foo anyway?" The room erupted in laughter and Brad stomped out of the room red–faced.

Brad often ate lunch at a Korean restaurant near work. One Tuesday he sat at the counter and ordered coffee and the shrimp special. The Korean waitress (who spoke very little English) said, "Yes." After two cups of coffee and still no lunch, Brad got the attention of the waitress and asked, "What about my shrimp special?" The waitress said, "Yes, yes." When Brad's half hour lunch–time was almost over, he asked the waitress again (in a rather loud voice), "Where's my shrimp special?" To which the waitress said, "Shrimp special Thursday, this Tuesday." Brad returned to the office with no lunch except coffee.

I must say one thing about Brad, though. He had values that rarely showed through, but when they did, you never forgot. For instance, when any coworker left our office for "greener pastures," we typically gathered after work at the local watering hole for a little farewell party. On one such occasion, I arrived to work the evening shift, and all of the day shift folks sauntered off to the little pub down the street. After an hour or so, Brad came back to the office and said, "Go have a drink with the group. I'll watch the office until you get back." I couldn't believe what I was hearing. I said, "But why would you do this for me?" He said simply, "Why not, you would do it for me." Never underestimate the power of living as an example to others, no matter how different or unreachable they may seem to be.

Going up?

Both of our children attended College in Kentucky. One year while moving our daughter into her dorm, I hauled load after load via hand truck and elevator. Since there was only one elevator in the building and all the parents were moving their daughters in at the same time, there was often a wait. If you haven't figured it out yet, my mind sometimes works in strange ways. To take advantage of those special moments, you have to abandon reason, logic, and lots of other things that slow you down.

I was on the second floor, leaning on the empty hand truck, waiting for the elevator to go down so I could pick up another load, when the doors opened and a father and mother of a student began to get out, saying, "Is this the third floor?" I said, "No, this is the second floor." They got back into the elevator, and as soon as the doors closed, I grabbed the hand truck and ran up the stairs to the third floor. I assumed the same position just outside the entrance to the elevator. As the doors opened, the same couple eyed me and said, "Isn't this the third floor?" I said, "No, this is still the second floor." They looked at me blankly for a moment and then I had to laugh and told them that this was indeed the third floor. Fortunately for me, they found this extremely funny, and the story of the prank spread quickly throughout the second and third floors. I later discovered that their daughter and my daughter were friends. I got a chance to talk to the couple later and they told me again how funny that prank was. (Whew; Dodged another bullet!)

No Pants

Every summer, our family travels to Illinois to visit Alice's family. This has been our ritual for quite a few years. Although we changed some aspects of the trip as we aged (like taking more than one day to drive the 730 miles), the basic trip still means fun and work combined.

In the early days of making this pilgrimage, I would work all day at my job and Alice would spend the day packing for the family and making sandwiches for the trip. When I got home, we packed the car and departed for Illinois. We began our journey about 6 p.m. and drove until midnight to 2 a.m., at which time we pulled into a rest stop for a couple of hours. We usually arrived about mid or late afternoon on the second day, and I was always exhausted.

Alice tried to have everything ready to throw into the car when I got home from work, and usually this worked great. On one trip however, I discovered when unpacking that I had no pants. I especially needed Jeans to work in, because I always helped around the farm and with Alice's father's electrical business.

The next day I donned a pair of Alice's blue jeans (which were big in one dimension and short in the other), and headed to town. The men's clothing store that I entered was definitely "upscale," and when I told the clerk that I needed some jeans, he began to look for the label on the jeans that I was wearing. I quickly said, "Oh, don't look at the size on these, they're my wife's." The look he gave me was hysterical, and I quickly realized that I needed to explain my situation to him, much to his enjoyment. I managed to buy a couple pairs of jeans in my size and the rest of our vacation went without a hitch.

Ten Cent Fix

Two coworkers, Gus and Ellen, lived in a condo and had a strange electrical problem. One circuit was dead and another friend of theirs had tried to help but he couldn't find the problem, so they asked me to take a look at it. Each apartment had its own meter and fuse panel. I traced the dead circuit back to the fuse box, but when I replaced the fuse, the circuit still had no electricity. I finally discovered there was a break between the main bus and the fuse socket, within the panel itself. I told them they needed a new main panel. I suggested they get an electrician to change it, as I had never done that before (and there wasn't a shutoff for the main panel), but they wanted me to do it. I finally agreed and purchased a new panel the same size as the existing one, but with circuit breakers, not fuses. Since the metal box was recessed, I couldn't pull the wires out of the box to remove it. I disconnected the supply wires from the main lugs then taped the bare ends with layers of electrical tape and friction tape. After disconnecting the load side of the panel, I carefully pulled the panel out of the wall bottom first, then the top, slipping it over the live wires. Everything went smoothly and soon the old panel was removed. I slipped the new box over the taped wires and fastened it to the wall. I then reconnected all the wires and everything worked including the circuit that was dead with the previous panel in place. Gus and Ellen were impressed and so was I.

Sometime later Gus asked me to go with them to look at a house they considered buying. I agreed and commented on some good and bad things about the house, most of which were personal preferences. They ended up buying the house, and then asked me to finish the basement for them. I'm not much of a carpenter, but I agreed and spent many evenings and weekends framing, hanging wallboard, wiring, and installing a suspended ceiling. The previous owner had built a closet at one end of the basement, closing in a "jog" in the wall. This closet was approximately three feet deep and eight feet wide. Gus didn't like the position of the door at the left end, so he asked me to move it to the middle of the space. I knocked out the door framing, filled in the space with studs and then cut out and framed the doorway in the center of the wall. After I completed the move, he decided he liked the door better where it was. So, I reversed the processed and put the door back in its original position.

After all of the basement framing was completed, Gus asked me to install a light on the basement stairs, with a switch at the top of the stairs. I put the light switch where he requested, but after installing the wallboard, he decided the switch should be located higher on the wall. I cut a new hole in the wallboard, moved the switch box, and put the cut–out from the new hole into the old hole, pasting it in with spackle. After spackling and painting over the old switch location, it was as though it never existed. Gus was fascinated by the "disappearing hole." Wallboard is neat stuff. Ellen reminded me many years later that whenever Gus wanted something changed, he would ask me if it was possible and I would say, "A little spackle, a little paint. No one will ever know."

One day, while I was busy on the basement construction, Gus asked if I would look at a ceiling fan that was wobbling, in the family room upstairs. Gus went elsewhere while I worked on the fan. One blade seemed lighter than the rest, so I got some cellophane tape, a dime from my pocket, and taped the dime on the top of the lighter blade, several inches from the fan motor. After a few adjustments of the dime's position, I had the fan running without any wobble whatsoever.

When Gus saw how smoothly the fan was running, he said, "How much do I owe you for fixing the fan?" I said, "Ten cents." He said, "Why ten cents?" I said, "Because I didn't have a penny."

Break Time

During my career, I spent many hours in various training classes learning about new technology, equipment, and even social skills (The reader can decide if they were successful or not). Most of the technical classes could put a wide–awake person into "drowsy" mode in a hurry! An outside contractor who was teaching one such class told us at the beginning of the class that he was presenting a lot of new information, so we should give him a sign if we needed a break.

My brother and I had recently been to a model train show where I purchased a lapel pin that was a model railroad crossing signal, complete with blinking red lights powered by a small battery.

As the instructor droned on and on, I could see everyone nodding, but not to the instructor's comments. I powered up the railroad crossing signal, which I had pinned onto my shirt pocket. That got his attention, but he didn't get the message! He stopped, looked at me and said, "Am I going too fast? Are you trying to tell me to slow down?" I said, "No, you wanted us to let you know when we needed a break, and I think this would be a good time for one." The class loved it, but the instructor looked pained that I had taken him at his word. He ignored me and kept going for a while longer. Don't say it if you don't mean it!

English?

Then there was the packet data transmission class. Packet was relatively new then, but is now used for the majority of data transmission. This class was also taught by a contractor, but one with an accent making it difficult to understand even with full attention to every word. To make matters worse, most of what he said was in acronyms.

At one point during a very complicated description of the seven layers of data, the instructor said a whole sentence that made absolutely no sense. The entire sentence was made up of unfamiliar acronyms. I finally lost it and started laughing. The instructor stopped and said, "What's so funny?" I said, "You just said a whole sentence and there wasn't an English word in it! It was all acronyms." I went on to explain that we weren't familiar with all the acronyms, and it would be better if he would tell us what the acronyms stood for as he used them. He ignored my suggestions and kept right on using acronyms. I was totally lost as was the rest of the class. Not one student asked a question at the end of each session and we all left silently when the class was over. Fortunately, this experience was not typical. Instructors were usually very good.

Whoopee Cushion

During the early 1970's, our company began hiring women to work in the once–all–male technician role. When two women joined our office, one of the male technicians immediately gave them male nicknames, which stuck for the duration of their job as technicians. Women working side–by–side on the job with men certainly changed the dynamics of the office. Even the practical jokes took a new turn, including one prank that involved a "whoopee cushion."

To keep skill levels in various job functions up–to–date, technicians rotated jobs within the office. At this particular time I worked in the circuit order department, which consisted of two pairs of side–by–side desks, one pair behind the other. One of the new female technicians sat directly in front of my desk, and several times I had tried to put a whoopee cushion on her chair without her seeing it. Unfortunately, she noticed it every time before she sat down. The chairs were metal, with vertical bars that began at the top of the back, but did not go all the way down to the seat. A horizontal metal bar terminated the vertical bars about four to five inches above the seat, leaving an open area at the base of the backrest.

After failing to fall for the prank on the third or fourth try, the female technician once again threw the whoopee cushion at me. As she turned to sit down, I took a chance and sailed cushion "Frisbee style" toward the opening on the lower part of her chair back. The shot was perfect. The cushion sailed through the opening and landed flat on the seat of her chair just as she put her full weight on it. The sound was absolutely marvelous. Everyone in the immediate area burst into laughter. She jumped up, red–faced with embarrassment, and threw the whoopee cushion at me again. I was surprised to get it back again, but I didn't dare push my luck. Persistence paid off, but once success had been achieved, the cushion was retired.

OJ

After fourteen years in an equipment office and two and a half years in a data center, I transferred to an engineering job in Virginia. My partner in engineering, Sindhu, was a young man from India. We had many interesting conversations and I found many opportunities to test his sense of humor. (He was a very amiable person with whom I enjoyed working.) Our shared cubicle was on the south side of the building against an outside wall consisting of very large windows. During the winter months when the sun was low in the sky, we were forced to close large vertical blinds as it got quite warm on our side of the building. The blinds also helped reduced glare from our computer screens.

One day I noticed a thin vertical sliver of sunlight slipping through the blinds and moving across my computer screen. I decided to time it. I put a sticky tab on my computer screen at the light's present location and then marked it one hour later. When I measured the distance between the two marks, I told Sindhu, "The sun is moving two inches per hour." Of course he would have none of this and said very seriously, "No, that is not true... See you are very much closer to the window than is the sun, and the sun is moving much faster than that. It just isn't true. You cannot measure the movement of the sun in that way." I tried my best not to laugh but I couldn't help it, and he finally realized that I was not serious. (Of course it isn't the sun that's moving anyway.)

Although we shared the common areas of our floor with three other engineering groups, our group owned a small refrigerator. The chore of cleaning out and defrosting the refrigerator rotated monthly between the management employees in our group. Since there were eight of us, there should never have been more than two months without the fridge being cleaned. Unfortunately, most of the people in my group refused to do it. When it was my turn, I discovered the ice in the freezer section was at least an inch thick. It hadn't been cleaned for probably six months, possibly a year.

I arrived at work the next day armed with a hair dryer, a small cooler and a determined resolve to complete the task. First I removed everything from the freezer and put it into the cooler. After removing most things, I noticed a broken glass bottle and "yellow ice" (not the same as yellow snow) all around it. I removed the pieces of the bottle (which I identified as a small orange juice bottle), including the neck with the lid still attached. I put the broken glass into the trash. I placed a pan under the freezer compartment and fired up the hair dryer, melting the ice and frost.

The defrosting and cleaning took most of the morning, but when done, the refrigerator looked great—especially the freezer compartment. I was a little upset however, that someone had put a glass bottle into the freezer. I assumed they just wanted to cool it quickly and had forgotten it was there, but when I asked the group, "Who put it there?" I got no response. I complained to Sindhu that I couldn't believe someone would put a glass bottle containing liquid into the freezer, but he said nothing. Later that day I again mentioned the broken bottle and the mess it made to Sindhu, and he practically yelled, "*I* put the bottle in there, and someone broke it!" I started to laugh and said, "No one broke the bottle, the liquid expanded when it froze and that's what broke the bottle." "No," he said, "Everyone knows that all things shrink when the temperature goes below freezing." I laughed again and said, "Everything except liquids." Sindhu was born and raised in India and knew only theory when it came to things freezing. He didn't believe me so I told him to look it up. The next day he admitted I was right. Although he hated to admit he was wrong, I think he was relieved that no one intentionally broke his bottle of orange juice. Theory never beats experience as a teacher.

Coffee Pot

The coffee pot was another office item that required regular cleaning. Even though I didn't drink coffee, I was on the list to clean the coffee pot. Coffee drinkers know how dirty a coffee pot can get when making coffee once a day and this pot was perking all day long, every day. It was gross!

I attacked this chore with the same diligence with which I had cleaned the refrigerator. In the morning I arrived with a bottle of white vinegar. After a couple pots of coffee were distributed to the thirsty—and sleepy—workers, the pot was empty. I chose this lull in activity around the area of the coffee pot to do a thorough job in cleaning it. I had learned that white vinegar will remove coffee and tea stains from glass and ceramic—and possibly other things—so I poured some into the glass coffee pot and sloshed it around sufficiently to clean the inside. I then dumped the vinegar out and wiped the inside of the pot with paper towels. To ensure I got all the vinegar out, I rinsed the pot with water and wiped it again with paper towels. It looked as good as new.

The outside of the machine was wiped clean with vinegar as well and then it was time to clean the inside of the coffee machine. I decided the only way to do this was to put some white vinegar into the coffee maker's water reservoir and turn it on. This would force the vinegar through the machine's plumbing as well as heat it, possibly allowing it to work even better.

Soon after the coffee maker began dripping vinegar, I was visited by people from near and as far away as the other end of the building, wondering what in the world I was doing to make all that smell. Apparently, some people don't enjoy the smell of vinegar and as a friend of mine used to say, "Nothing goes like stink!" I learned that heated (and maybe vaporized) vinegar creates much more smell than does liquid poured from a bottle. I'm afraid I haven't a final answer on the results of the cleaning process, as the procedure was prematurely suspended by popular demand. (I think it would have worked great though)

Bubble Wrap

Everyone knows how great it is to pop the bubbles in packing material. There are big bubbles and little bubbles. I prefer the small ones. The engineering offices were merely cubicles in an open floor. After leaving the engineering department, I worked in a small office area containing only 5 employees. Cubicle walls were five feet high and provided some sense of privacy while working.

One of my responsibilities involved ordering, receiving and installing software and equipment for our small group. A carton arrived one day while the boss was out and after opening the box, everyone grabbed a piece of bubble wrap and began popping it. After a short while the popping ceased and we got back to work.

One of my coworkers, Joan, resided two cubicles from me. I casually walked past her cubicle and noticed that she was engrossed in her computer screen. I quietly slipped into her cubicle placing a small sheet of un–popped bubbles on the floor behind her chair. She didn't notice me at all. I returned to my desk and everything was quiet for about five minutes. Suddenly, I heard a rapid–fire popping noise like a machine gun or Chinese fire crackers and a scream! Joan had pushed her chair back from her desk and rolled the wheels over the bubbles. It startled her considerably—and the rest of us too! I suddenly realized that Joan could have had a heart attack, so I didn't do that again. Andy Capp (my favorite British cartoon character) said, "As I get older, I find myself doing more and more for the last time, and less and less for the first time." That's life.

Footprints to Nowhere

The office where the bubble wrap incident occurred was built on a raised floor, so that cabling could be run under the floor for computers, phones, and other equipment. This required walking up a ramp to enter any of the office areas from the elevator lobby. At the end of the elevator hallway, separate ramps led to office areas on the left and right. The ramp on the right led to a landing from which our office was entered and a second door led to other office areas. The ramp was only one half the width of the hallway, so there existed a narrow lobby–level hallway next to the ramp, leading to a blank wall. Industrial grade short–nap carpet, made for high traffic areas, covered the hallway floors. Each night the cleaning crew buffed the carpet which created a slight pattern on the carpet surface making it possible to see footprints, especially in the less traveled areas. This gave me an idea to create a little mystery.

My work day began an hour earlier than everyone else. One morning before anyone else had arrived, I carefully stepped backwards to the dead–end wall next to the ramp leading to our office, then I retraced my steps carefully so that only one set of footprints appeared, supposedly leading out of the wall. I did this on a regular basis for a while, but never heard any comments. Surely someone must have noticed, especially the cleaning crew. I often wondered if they looked for a secret door.

The Secretary

One of my positions with the company involved meeting with telecommunications personnel from government agencies. My boss informed me one day that he and I would attend a meeting in the Pentagon. I knew two people at the Pentagon, but had lost track of one of them. The other man, Virgil, reported directly to the Secretary of the Navy. I decided to mention Virgil to my boss and find out if we could take a few moments to visit Virgil's office and perhaps even meet the Secretary of the Navy.

My boss was always interested in meeting important people. In fact, he was very conscious of a person's position and title. I expected him to jump at the chance to meet someone as important as the Secretary of the Navy. That's why I was shocked when I mentioned the possible visit and my boss said, "I'm not wasting my time seeing some secretary!"

I was at a loss for words, so I simply said, "Ok," and let it go. I said nothing more about it to my boss, but I mentioned the strange response to my coworker, Joan, whose husband was a Rear Admiral. She was surprised by his response as well. The Secretary of the Navy is Commander of both the United States Navy and the United States Marines, and reports directly to the "Commander in Chief"—the

President. *"A quick–tempered man does foolish things, and a crafty man is hated. The simple inherit folly, but the prudent are crowned with knowledge."* (Proverbs 14:17–18)

Golf Cart Reverse

Golf course personnel are very trusting. Few of them check to see if you have a driver's license, are sane, or have previously driven small carts into ponds. In order to rent a cart you simply pay, sign a little waiver vowing that you've read all the fine print and agree to everything (does anyone ever really read that stuff?), and then you can not only cause mayhem and havoc with a little white ball shooting off at obtuse angles like a bullet, but you can drive willy–nilly about the landscape, while other golfers feel perfectly safe in the serene setting.

One day Carey (Alice's niece) and I went to a local golf course to play a round of golf. I had only played a few times in my life and had driven a cart only a few times. We loaded our clubs onto a cart, and when we got the call to go to the first tee, I attempted to get the cart to move forward. This should have been a simple matter, as there is only a gas pedal, a brake, a direction lever and a key. Pressing on the gas pedal should start the engine and increase the speed. No matter what I did however, including choking the engine and turning the key off and on, I could not get the engine running. Thinking the cart might not be in gear properly, I moved the lever from forward to reverse, then to forward again. I still couldn't get it to move. I turned the key off and on again. After playing with the forward/reverse lever a few more times, the cart roared to life and bolted. Unfortunately, the moment this cantankerous cart chose to move was the moment that I had the lever in reverse! Our cart lurched into the one behind us. As I turned around to apologize, I noticed that the young man in the cart had a very surprised look on his face. That's not all that was on his face, or his shirt, or his pants. He had been drinking a large soda from a cup without a lid and was now wearing some of it. He said some very bad words to no one in particular, and headed for the clubhouse to rinse the soda out of his shirt, and perhaps wash his face as well. I intended to apologize and some form of apology did escape my lips, but alas, my gut reaction was to laugh. I don't think my apology sounded sincere through all the laughter. The entire situation was extremely funny, except to the guy wearing the soda of course.

Cooking

I'm not a cook. Let's get that straight from the very beginning! However, every once in a while I'm called upon to make a meal on the grill. My kids trust me, but they have been known to be a little tentative about the ingredients I might use.

Perhaps I should explain my theory about eating. God made *ALL* food and I think He called it all *good*. I agree, and therefore I like everything. The members of my family often think I have weird taste in food, however.

I guess it all began when I was a little tyke. I loved rhubarb sauce. I don't remember this part, but my sister–in–law, Lucy, who was in the first grade with me, reminds me that I would bring rhubarb sauce to school in a glass jar. She says I could never open the jar, so the teacher would open it for me. Lucy says she couldn't imagine anyone *wanting* the jar opened. I also love Brussels sprouts, spinach, sauerkraut, and lots of other wonderful food.

A trick instigated by Alice and her sister–in–law proves my point. I made travel arrangements to attend a work–related class in a small town near Chicago, which was a short distance from Alice's brother Dean and his wife Lilly. When I informed Lilly of my plans, she immediately invited me to eat with them when I was in the area and then quickly added, "Is there anything you don't like?" I couldn't think of anything at the time. In the weeks before the trip, she asked several times if there was anything I didn't eat. I couldn't think of a thing.

The evening finally arrived for my visit. After catching up on the family news for a while, the table was set and we sat down to supper. On my plate was an upside–down bowl. Lilly said it was a special surprise. After the prayer I was allowed to remove the bowl and eat. When I lifted the bowl, I uncovered a pile of small red radishes! I picked one up, popped it in my mouth and ate it, then I picked up another one and Lilly said, "You even eat radishes! Alice said you didn't like radishes! I guess there really isn't anything you don't like." The look on her face when I ate the first radish was precious. The joke was on her.

Radishes aren't my favorite and I don't often eat them (there's too much better food available), but I don't mind them. I'd rather have an onion sandwich—sliced onion, bread, butter, and salt.

As I said, I like everything. So, when I make something simple like hamburgers on the grill, it becomes a complicated process. No two batches of burgers are ever the same. Anything in the kitchen cabinet is fair game. For instance, I might add a little steak sauce, a little brandy (we usually don't have that so anything with alcohol will do), honey, parsley, garlic, catsup, mustard, vinegar, salt, pepper, cinnamon, nutmeg, bread crumbs, and other assorted goodies. If it resides in our kitchen—and is edible—it might find its way into a burger on my grill. I discovered early on that if I didn't tell the kids what was in their burgers until *after* they ate them, all was well. They always liked the burgers, but it did seem to make them a little more apprehensive the next time, if I revealed what I had put in them.

I don't normally watch cooking shows on TV, but one day I watched a young chef make a "world class hamburger," as he called it. I had been doing it all wrong! Not the ingredients, but how I mixed them together. The first order of business is to use ground beef with SOME fat. The lean stuff just doesn't cook up nice and juicy and tender according to the chef. The second tip is; don't smash the ground beef and squeeze it and mix the ingredients into the meat with your hands! Be gentle, and *fold* the ingredients into the meat, but not too much. The ingredients will cook into the meat even if they are not evenly distributed.

Even the bun was an interesting concept on this cooking show. The chef took a small oval loaf of bread—shaped like a blunt–ended football—and cut off both ends (large enough to use the ends for the sandwich). He then removed some of the inside bread from each end piece to make a pocket. When the hamburger was ready he placed it in one of the bread ends, then added lettuce, tomato, and other goodies. Finally, the opposite end of the bread loaf was placed on top. Neither the hamburger nor anything else slid out when he took a big bite. I've tried this method of making hamburgers and it works quite well. The hamburger tastes fantastic when prepared in this way. I agree with the chef; It is a "world class hamburger." Although my family members are still leery about the ingredients, they like my burgers even better now.

For dessert, there is nothing better (or easier) than a baked apple. Take an apple—one for each person—and cut it into quarters (or smaller wedges), removing the core. Sprinkle the inside of the apple with sugar and cinnamon, then place the quarters together again and wrap with aluminum foil. When you remove the hamburgers or steaks from the grill, replace them with the apples. By the time the main course is done the apples will be ready and dessert can be served. This, even I can handle.

Trick or Treat

The party

Halloween is a special time for people who enjoy being a little different and being someone—or something—else for a while. I always enjoyed Halloween growing up, but while working, I discovered the joy of owning a rubber mask. I eventually bought three masks; an old man mask, an old woman mask, and finally Chewbacca the "Wookie." The masks were somewhat expensive, but the "laughs–per–dollar" made them worth every cent.

My favorite recollection of Halloween is the time Alice and I attended a friend's costume party. We drove several miles to the party and decided to "stay in character" the whole time. Alice dressed up as an old man and I dressed up as an old woman, both using the realistic rubber masks. Because Alice is much shorter than I am, we looked like an odd couple. Alice drove and parked the car up the street from our destination so we wouldn't be recognized by the vehicle. She got out and hobbled around the car to open my door and help me out. We noticed a couple walking down the street toward us, still some distance away, but when we exited the car they stopped.

We commented to each other about how strange that seemed as we walked to our friend's house.

At the door we were greeted by our friend, who was dressed as one of the sand people from Star Wars, complete with glowing red eyes. He could not guess who we were. In fact, no one could guess who we were. They couldn't imagine what couple they knew where the man was short and the woman was tall.

Shortly after we arrived and were mingling with the guests, another couple appeared at the door. As the door opened they both threw open their bath robes, exposing plastic "naked body" costumes. From a distance they looked pretty darn real! The entire group laughed hysterically!

After everyone had revealed their identity, we shared our experience when parking the car and walking to the party. The "naked" couple told us they were the ones we saw walking down the street, stopping when we got out of the car. They were afraid that if the old man and woman saw the naked body costumes they might have a heart attack. That's why they waited for us to walk down the street first. I guess our characters worked quite well.

Chewie

Chewbacca is a character in the original Star Wars movie. When I saw the Chewbacca mask in the costume shop I just had to have it. Alice had made a bear costume for a local theater group, out of brown furry material and the costume fit me perfectly. I cut out two shoe print sized pieces of ridged foam and glued them to the bottoms of an old pair of sneakers with "Shoe Goo." This made me four inches taller. I then covered the sneakers and foam with furry material to make them look like furry feet. I found hairy rubber "paws" at a costume store to complete the outfit. No one ever figured out who was in the Chewbacca costume. I had fun being "Chewy," but never laughed as much as when the "old man" and "old woman" attended the Halloween party.

Scary

Can a frightful scare shorten someone's life? I certainly hope not.

One Halloween I took the old man mask to work with me at a data center and occasionally put it on to walk around the building. The only other part of the "costume" was an old green button up sweater.

The mainframe computers were located in huge air–conditioned rooms (two floors). Noise generated by the equipment made it very easy to sneak up on someone. Equipment areas were normally devoid of people, but on this particular day a vendor was at one of the large machines talking on a pillar mounted telephone. I donned the mask and worked my way ever–so–quietly to the opposite side of the equipment, which was about chest high. When I was directly opposite the vendor, still below his line of sight, I slowly rose as though riding an elevator and looked him in the eye. We were about four feet apart. He sort of screamed that "little girl" scream (you know—the scream that could break a wine glass), and kept jerking backwards staccato–like until he ran out of telephone cord. I was almost ashamed that I caused so much fear. Almost.

Book 2 – Extraordinary From the Ordinary

Chapter I: Drawn In

The Hound of Heaven

C. S. Lewis, Francis Thompson, and other writers talk about the "Hound of Heaven," meaning God's Holy Spirit. God pursues us continually, with more patience and love than we can ever imagine. I have come to believe this and see that God has been actively working in my life, sometimes in ways that I didn't appreciate at the time.

My first work location with the communications company got very stressful as fewer and fewer people remained to do the same amount of work. From an initial group of seven people in the carrier section of the office, I became the sole remaining workforce. Not only that, but my supervisor was in another office (a much bigger office in Washington D.C.), and I was put on their call–out list as well as the call out list for my own work location. I was on call twenty–four hours a day seven days a week. Every time the telephone rang at home, I literally felt my stomach churn. I was physically sick every other week with vomiting and diarrhea. Eventually I went to our family doctor and although he conducted several tests, he found nothing wrong with me. Just before our scheduled vacation to Ocean City, Maryland, the doctor advised me to stay away from alcohol and spicy or rich food. Who can go to the beach without eating crabs and pizza and drinking beer?

Our family spent one week at the beach with another couple and their daughter, then stayed in a neighbor's condo for a second week.

I relaxed. I ate crabs and pizza, and drank beer. I felt better than I had for a long time. The stress was gone and so were the stomach and intestinal problems.

After our two–week vacation, I returned to work and although I never again experienced the stomach and intestinal problems, it was likely due to a change in location and type of work soon after our vacation. I began a totally new type of job, working in a billing data center, but for the same company. Even though I felt out of my element in the data center, I enjoyed the work and people very much. The drive to work was easier, parking was free and the job came with a pay increase. I thought I had it made. After two and a half years however, the data center closed and I was forced to look for another position. I couldn't believe that the job I enjoyed so much was going away.

There were four other data centers that I might have transferred to: one in Georgia, one in California, one in Massachusetts, and one in Florida. Alice's brother lived near Atlanta, so while visiting him we stopped by the data center to check it out. The building was new and very nice, as were the people. I had worked with some of them over the telephone and knew one woman who had transferred to this data center from the one I was now forced to leave. She highly recommended the area, and told me how much she liked it there.

Alice and I loved the homes and people in the area, but our children didn't want to move, and Alice did not like the hot weather. If there is any place worse than Washington D.C. for humidity in the summer, it's Atlanta. For those "Gone With The Wind" fans, you may recall a reference to "the red clay of Tara." There are large areas of red clay around Atlanta, and it just seems to radiate the heat and humidity. Even though I didn't know it at the time, our decision not to move was the right one. In time, some of the other data centers began closing as well, and I might very well have had to move again soon.

After trying in vain to find work in Maryland, I finally accepted an engineering position in Virginia (still with the same company). For the first time in my career, I was now "management". I did get a raise, but my commute doubled and involved quite a bit of time on the Washington beltway. At the time, the American Legion Memorial Bridge (sometimes misnamed the Cabin John Bridge) was being widened, so my commute was sometimes one–and–a–half hours long in each direction.

I was not happy with my new work location, but now realize it was probably the best thing that could have happened to me. I told Alice that I would like audio tapes to listen to during the commute to and from work. She asked me what I might like to listen to, and I said, "Maybe the Bible on tape." She purchased the Bible on cassette tape from Hosanna Ministries in Texas, and I listened to them over and over and over! I became so anxious to hear the next segment, I just couldn't wait to get into the car again and get out in rush–hour traffic! I've heard about "a hunger and thirst for the Lord," and I found out what that meant. I listened to the entire Bible (Old and New Testaments) at least twice and New Testament no less than 20 times.

One day while listening to the Psalms, I heard, *"He will cover you with his feathers, and under his wings you will find refuge; his faithfulness will be your shield and rampart."* (Psalm 91:4) I no more than heard the Scripture, when I looked up to see in the sky, a cloud stretching from the middle of the sky above me to the far western horizon—shaped perfectly like an outstretched wing, feathers and all. As I contemplated what just happened, I again looked up another mile down the road and saw a cloud from the eastern horizon to the western horizon—shaped like a perfect wing! I knew immediately that God can be any size He wants to be. There is no limit to what God can do. I also knew this was no co–incidence and began using the term "God–incident." I also knew that God, although unlimited in all aspects, communicates with us as a friend. One–on–one!

On another day, I was returning home after a long day and after several days of rainy weather, when I noticed the end of the cloud cover just above the horizon in the west. The sun was just going down, but as it did, the bottom of the cloud cover was illuminated and the entire sky became golden in appearance. I immediately began thinking this must be what heaven looks like, and I began praising God.

The clincher

In 1989, a preacher/evangelist from Florida conducted a healing service in a small church near our home. my evening began like this: It was a Friday night, and after a particularly hectic day and even more frustrating drive home in rush–hour traffic, I plopped into my recliner chair and said, "Don't bother me all evening, I'm not moving from this chair!" Then the phone rang. I heard only one side of the conversation, but it was enough to get my interest. "Service... Barry... Healing... 7 o'clock... Chapel..." I kept trying to interject, "What is it? Where is it? How long does it last?" After Alice hung up the phone, she said, "There is a healing service tonight at 7pm, but you said you weren't interested in going anywhere." I said "I'd like to check this out, but if the service is longer than one hour, I'm out of there!"

So we went. I saw quite a few people that I knew, and as we sang praise songs and worshipping, I looked around to take in this new experience. I knew about worship services—I grew up in the Evangelical United Brethren Church, which merged with the Methodist Church and became the United Methodist Church. I was familiar with quiet, sit–down–and–behave type of worship, but this was different. Hands were raised, bodies were swaying, some people were crying, and I stood there with my eyes wide open. After a time of singing, Barry began speaking. I don't remember what he said, but it was obvious that the Spirit of God was present. He mentioned a specific problem or ailment then called the person forward as they acknowledged their need. When he placed a hand on them and commanded healing in the name of Jesus, most fell backward, caught by a friend or helper and lowered gently onto the carpet. When the person got up, they seemed affected by the experience. All claimed they were healed. All seemed different...more at peace.

One woman, whom we knew, had MS (Multiple Sclerosis) and was in a special testing program at NIH due to the rapidly progressing disease. She went forward for healing, and just like most of the others, PLOP! Down on the floor she went! After a while, she got up and returned to her seat. I continued watching as one person after another went forward to receive healing.

Alice eventually looked at her watch and realized it was time for her to pick up our kids from a birthday party. I said, "Go ahead," and moved out of her way. I wasn't going to leave now! The service continued a while longer, but then the evangelist said, "If you want healing, come forward now. When I'm done, I'm done." When no one responded, he dismissed us and turned his back to us facing the cross in the front of the church.

I was exiting the church along with other people when Alice returned with our two children. I told Alice that the service was over, but she said, "I'm going in any way!" I followed her to see what would happen. She walked up to the evangelist (who still had his back to us), and said, "It isn't fair! I came for healing tonight, but I had to leave to pick up my children, and now I've been told that the service is over!" Barry turned around and said, "You came for healing, and healing you shall have!" Alice explained to him that she had a really bad headache and when she drove, she had to close one eye because her head hurt so much. She didn't tell him about the cough that had been plaguing her for a long time. She probably didn't think about it. He placed his hand on her forehead, commanding she be healed in Jesus' name, and down she went, onto the floor, flat on her back. The evangelist looked at a friend of Alice's and said, "You're her friend, put your hand on her stomach." So the lady kneeled down and placed her hand on Alice's stomach. She said it was as stiff as a board.

After a while, Alice opened her eyes and sat up. She said it was the strangest thing; while she was lying there, she could feel warmth start at her toes and move through her body to her head. When the warmth exited her head, both the headache and the cough were gone! Hallelujah! The evangelist said she would be healed and she was! I looked at my watch and couldn't believe we had been there 3 hours! I'm sure glad I didn't leave after one hour.

The next night, Barry returned for another healing service. You couldn't keep me away now! I saw many of the same people, but some new ones also. Our friend with MS was there and gave her testimony, saying she had a good night's sleep for the first time in years. She didn't feel weak, her head was clear and she felt completely healed.

We found out later that NIH had released her from the special study program she was in because they saw NO MS ACTIVITY! Praise the Lord!

Up Close and Personal

After my encounter with the evangelist, God was no longer some distant, unreachable entity. No longer were prayers half–hearted words spoken into a void. I knew God was real and that He hears every word. God is as near as our next breath; close enough to hear a whisper and know even our thoughts.

Alice's friend Jody purchased How to Heal the Sick, a videotape produced by Charles and Frances Hunter. Jody, Alice, and another friend watched the videotape on Saturday mornings, breaking the six–hour tape into two–hour segments. After I heard about them watching the first video segment, I asked to take part in the second session. The following Saturday, we gathered at Jody's home, and the session began.

We sat on the edge of our chairs and tried to take notes, paying close attention to every word. After watching Charles and Frances explain how to command healing for a particular part of the body, we stopped the tape and practiced. I believe God had me there for this session on purpose, because it addressed precisely what I needed.

When I was around fourteen years old, I spent the night with a friend, Dave, and we camped out in his side yard. We were running around his yard after dark when I fell on some broken cement around the old well pump, cutting my knee severely, and evidently chipping a bone, which I didn't know until years later. I'm still amazed that I tried out for track in High School, served in the USAF four years, and had no problem with the knee. Shortly after I was discharged from the service, however, I was stretching and exercising, when I "kicked" my left leg out and something "snapped," but I still felt nothing out of the ordinary.

Through the years that followed, however, I noticed more and more that my knee would lock in the bent position while walking. Occasionally, when I tried to step with my left leg, I could not straighten it. I often had to grab something to keep from falling. I saw two doctors, neither of which could find a problem, even with X–rays.

After I met Alice and found that she knew an orthopedic surgeon who specialized in athletic injuries (and had operated on her ankle after she smashed it falling on ice), I went to see her surgeon. After an examination, he told me that the muscles in my left leg had atrophied from not using it as much as the other and that there certainly was something wrong with the knee. I had lost movement in the knee, not being able to straighten it completely, nor bend it fully. He scheduled an exploratory surgery.

It was 1973, the year Alice and I were married and bought our house, that the doctor operated on my knee. He removed the bone chip which he discovered floating around in my knee, scraped and shaped the bone and cartilage, and flushed out all the little balls of cartilage—from microscopic to BB size—that were being ground up by the bone chip and joint. The four hour surgery was successful, and after 8 weeks of recovery I was walking just fine, although I have never since been able to bend that knee fully.

While the surgery was successful, within a few years the knee became arthritic. It hurt constantly, especially when the weather was about to change. My knee was a good barometer, always hurting just before (and during) a change in the weather.

Then in 1976, when Alice was eight months pregnant with our son, we had freezing rain overnight that covered everything with a layer of ice. As I got ready to go to work, I noticed our neighbor's car had turned sideways at the end of their driveway. With a ditch in front and behind the car, it was going to be nearly impossible to drive the car out of this predicament. I ran across our lawn to help my neighbor, but when I stepped onto their driveway, my foot flew up in front of me and I fell with my back arched and my feet in the air. I landed on my back and heard a loud "pop" and felt a sharp pain in the upper portion of my back—between the shoulder blades. I lay there for a while, but then slowly got up and gingerly walked back to my house. I felt as though someone had hit me in the middle of the back with a knuckle.

After the ice melted I drove to the hospital, where they told me (after X–rays) one vertebra had been crushed, much like a soda can crumpled on one side. The hospital admitted me overnight for observation and the next day I was fitted with a back brace, which I wore for eight weeks.

From the time of the fall itself, the initial pain remained. It was not a severe pain, but was constant day and night. The doctor also told me that the injury would no doubt become arthritic over the years (I didn't know enough to refuse to accept that statement back then). True to his words, a few years later my back became extremely painful, especially during a night of tossing and turning, trying to sleep. Sometimes the pain was so severe that I could not sit up to get out of bed. I often had to slide to the edge of the bed and carefully swing my legs over the side of the bed, roll onto my side, then put my feet on the floor as I pushed myself to a sitting position with my arm. After I was up and moving for a while, the pain settled down to its normal constant annoyance. Over the next ten years, I was treated by three different chiropractors. Each brought a measure of relief, but the pain was a constant presence.

Approximately 13 years after my back injury, and 29 years after my knee injury, Alice and I and another friend sat watching the healing video at Jody's home. The first segment that we saw covered legs, knees, ankles and feet. After stopping the video tape to practice, I explained the situation with my knee. One of the women—practicing what the tape had just instructed—commanded healing in the name of Jesus. I instantly felt the ache in my knee disappear, never to return! (No more weather forecasting!)

After taking turns praying for each other so that we all received practice, the videotape resumed. The next subject dealt with backs, so I offered my back as a test. Again, one of the women commanded healing in the name of Jesus, speaking according to the suggestions on the tape, and the pain left immediately! After more than 13 years of constant pain, my knee and back were pain free! Although I have since experienced back pains occasionally, none have been the same as the one that was healed on that day.

Fourteen years after my back was healed, I somehow injured my lower back, which made it difficult to swing a golf club. I played golf with friends anyway, but toward the end of the round, my back hurt so much I didn't think I would be able to finish. For the next few days I didn't sleep well because I couldn't get comfortable. During a Bible study at church, I related a few of the miracles from my past and when I stood up to leave I felt much less pain in my back, but it was certainly still there. During that night, the pain again caused me to wake up several times.

The next morning, I needed to remove the rear seats from our minivan and drive 25 miles to load several heavy items into the van to take to a church yard sale, along with three sections of steel tower, each ten feet long, which had to be lifted onto the roof rack and tied down. I had no help. I didn't know how I was going to do all of that with my back hurting. Before I began the task at hand, Alice gently put her arms around me with her hands lightly on my back, said, "In the name of Jesus, I command the muscles, tendons, ligaments, and nerves to relax and allow the vertebrae and disks to go into their proper position." My back popped! (I was just standing there, and she wasn't pushing on my back at all!) We both heard it and I felt it, and the pain was GONE! I bent over, twisted, and moved with no pain! I was able to remove the seats from the van, Drive the 25 miles and load the inside of the minivan, put three tower sections and a twenty–two foot wooden extension ladder on the roof of the minivan, deliver them to the church and unload everything! I not only had no pain, but I felt stronger than I had in years! Not many items sold, including the tower sections, so I put them back onto the roof of the van, loaded up the inside of the van, and when I got home I unloaded everything and carried the three tower sections around the house to the back yard. I did all this with NO PAIN! The next golf game was a disaster on the score card, but I played with absolutely no pain.

The experience of our first healing service and then our personal experiences gave us unbridled joy and enthusiasm. You've no–doubt heard that being a Christian is boring. Let me tell you *that is a lie*! There is no greater excitement or joy than seeing someone healed by the power of God (especially when that person is you!). Why else would crowds follow Jesus? *"Then Peter said, "Silver or gold I do not have, but what I have I give you. In the name of Jesus Christ of Nazareth, walk." Taking him by the right hand, he helped him up, and instantly the man's feet and ankles became strong. He jumped to his feet and began to walk. Then he went with them into the temple courts, walking and jumping, and praising God. When all the people saw him walking and praising God, they recognized him as the same man who used to sit begging at the temple gate called Beautiful, and they were filled with wonder and amazement at what had happened to him."* (Acts 3:6–10)

Once we saw the miracles and knew they were REAL, there was no stopping us. We laid hands on and prayed for anyone and everyone who told us their problems. We didn't just say, "I'll pray for you," and then go away. We prayed for them on the spot! At work, in the grocery store, everywhere we went. We began seeing miracles every day. We called each other often and told about the miracles we witnessed. We soon discovered there were so many we couldn't remember them all. Some miracles, however, will remain with us forever!

Janet

One miracle etched in my memory is about our friend Janet. She attended an evening Bible study with us, and one night she arrived hunched over and in obvious pain. She could not straighten up. Janet said she almost didn't come because of the pain but she knew this was where she needed to be.

Janet's doctor had diagnosed her condition as Osteoporosis. Tests indicated bone mass decline in her hip and back, causing excruciating pain. I'm not sure if anyone else was aware of Janet's condition, but I certainly wasn't, and I felt very sympathetic to her obvious pain. (Seeing some people healed makes one want to see everyone healed!)

God heals in His time and His time is perfect. Janet suffered through the Bible study for a full hour or more, as no one felt led to lay hands on her and speak a word of healing. After the Bible study ended and refreshments were announced, we (or God) decided it was time for Janet to be healed. Some people went to another room to enjoy dessert, but our core healing group remained with Janet.

One person laid hands on Janet, facing her, while the rest of the small group crowded around her. The person facing Janet bound the spirit of Osteoporosis in Jesus' name, commanded healing in Jesus' name, and Janet fell over backwards. She was caught by one of our group and placed gently on the floor. Janet lay there as though sleeping. Since the living room was quite small, we had to step over her to get to the next room for coffee and dessert. Several minutes later, as we all sat around the living room with Janet lying in the middle of the floor, she finally began to stir. We helped her to her feet and she stood up tall and straight! As tears formed in her eyes, she told us that she had NO PAIN! Subsequent tests revealed that her bone deterioration had ceased and in fact, she was actually gaining bone mass. Hallelujah!

Chapter II: The Power of Darkness

Lessons in Spiritual Matters

The city of Allentown was familiar to me in name only. I had never been there even though I grew up in Pennsylvania. Around 1990, Charles and Frances Hunter advertised a three–day training session in Allentown, culminating in a healing service at a local arena. Alice, our two children and I, along with four friends, made plans to attend.

After work on Thursday evening our family loaded up our Toyota Camry and began driving to Allentown. All went well until we followed a route with sharp jogs and turns in local towns. Although we diligently looked for route signs, we found ourselves lost and our map didn't show enough detail to lead us back to the proper route. After frustration set in, we prayed and suddenly found the correct road again. This happened more than once. We should have seen this as an omen of what was to come.

Our family finally arrived at the motel where we had three rooms reserved, one for our family and two for our four friends, who would arrive separately. The motel was old and seemed very dark and spooky. The layout was strange, with several rows of rooms scattered around the property, seemingly at random. Although we thought this place seemed strange, Alice and I went to check in leaving our children in the car. As soon as we got to the desk, the clerk said, "You need to go to another motel. We've lost one leg of our main power, and only half of the rooms have any power at all." Because our longer than expected travel time had already made us late for the first night of activities, Alice said, "We don't have time to look for another motel and we have reservations here. By the time we get back here tonight, the power may be fixed. Just give us our room and we'll drop off our suitcases and come back later." The clerk finally agreed, so we drove across the parking lot to the correct section, found our room number and brought all the suitcases into the room. In preparation for being there the whole weekend, Alice unpacked her suitcase putting everything into drawers and hanging items in the closet. There was one working light in the room. I decided to wait and unpack when I got back. After putting everything into the room we drove to the church, where the weekend activities had already begun.

When we arrived at the church, I locked the car and we entered the church and found seats with our friends. I couldn't help but notice the size and layout of the church. It was more like a theater, complete with a large stage and three studio TV cameras on dollies. I thought to myself, "It sure would be nice to operate one of those again." (I hadn't operated a studio camera since 1963, but I had spent many years videotaping weddings, plays and other events using smaller video cameras.)

We began to relax as we enjoyed praise, worship, testimonies, and the presence of our friends. All too soon the evening activities ended and we returned to our car for the return trip to the motel. When I arrived at the car, it was unlocked. I commented to Alice that I knew I had locked the car. This was before remote controls were available, so locking was accomplished by turning a key in the driver's door and that locked the rest of the doors as well. She said, "You probably just thought you locked the car." I practically yelled, "I *did* lock the car." It had been a long day and we were all tired, but I *knew* I had locked the car.

We arrived at the motel late and tired but decided to stop by the desk and ask for additional towels and washcloths for the four of us. When the clerk asked for our room number, she said, "Oh... You'll have to move to another room. In order to have full power to part of the motel the power company had to switch the power from the section of rooms that you are in." She gave us the key to another room and we returned to our now totally dark room to repack all the clothes that Alice had so diligently put away. After repacking Alice's suitcase and loading the car we drove to another section of the motel and parked. I opened the door to the new room and as the four of us, suitcases in hand, stepped through the doorway; we were startled by the appearance and smell of the room. A small table in the middle of the room was covered with overflowing ashtrays and empty beer bottles. Even the floor was littered with beer bottles and the room reeked of stale cigarette smoke. We retreated hastily to the front desk once again.

When Alice and I explained to the desk clerk what we found, she didn't believe us! I told her she could check it out for herself, but we could not stay in that room! She reluctantly gave us the key to another room. It was now past midnight and we were obviously a little irritated.

Once again we drove to our new room, and again in another section of the motel property. This time the room seemed in good shape. All the lights worked. The plumbing worked. We carried the luggage into the room and Alice unpacked and put things away as before. I decided (again) to leave my bags packed and remove things as necessary. Once settled in I locked the door. Well, at least I *tried* to lock the door. There was no locking the door. Try as we might, neither Alice nor I could get the lock to work. I finally said, "I'm not going to worry about it. I'm going to sleep." Alice agreed, so we fastened the slide chain on the door, asked God to keep us safe, and went to bed. What a day!

Friday morning looked better. The sun was shining, birds were singing, and it was a fresh new day. After breakfast, we drove to the church for the first full day of activities. I parked the car, waited for Alice and the kids to get out, and locked the car making sure it was locked. We again found seats with our friends, though not in the front rows, which we preferred. We just couldn't seem to get there early enough to get a front row seat.

The morning program went by quickly and we enjoyed the speakers, lessons, and worship. Lunch was an hour–and–a–half so that everyone present had time to drive to a restaurant, eat, and then return. My family and our four friends decided to eat together. When I arrived at my car, I once again found the car unlocked! Alice said, "Oh, you must have left it unlocked again." This time I *DID* yell, "I did *NOT* leave the car unlocked. I locked it and checked to make sure it was locked before we went into the church." I searched the car quickly, but found no sign of forced entry, or anything missing (there wasn't anything in the car to steal anyway.)

Our group of eight headed to the nearest highway in two cars and drove east looking for a family–style restaurant. We found one a few miles away and stopped in for lunch. Service was a little slow, but not intolerable. After lunch we retraced our directions but for some strange reason missed our exit leading to the church. Both cars had to proceed to the next exit and turn around. By the time we arrived back at the church we were late... once again. We quickly parked. As I locked the car, I told Alice and our kids, "Ok, you see me lock the car. You see that the locking buttons are all down. You see that I cannot open the door." They all agreed that the car was indeed locked.

Because we were late returning, all of us had to crawl over people to get to our seats. Once seated, we again enjoyed the program, laughing at the humorous stories, learning from the instructional parts, and crying at the testimonies. Before we knew it, the afternoon session was over and it was again time to join our friends for a meal.

When I returned to my car, I found it unlocked again. This time, we simply laughed. Alice, our kids, and I, *knew* that we had left the car *locked.* This time I had witnesses. We had been unaware until this time, of the power of spiritual forces. This was indeed becoming a weekend of learning.

"For our struggle is not against flesh and blood, but against the rulers, against the authorities, against the powers of this dark world and against the spiritual forces of evil in the heavenly realms." (Ephesians 6:12)

Our two–car caravan arrived at a small restaurant located on the upper floor of an old house. Our group of eight was seated quickly, and we felt certain we would be back at the church in plenty of time for the evening session. After several minutes of talking among ourselves about the day's activities we realized no one had come to our table yet. We began to watch for a waitress and noticed that every table was being served except ours. Fifteen minutes went by. Thirty minutes went by. Finally, we got the attention of a waitress and asked if we could get some service. She apologized, took our drink order and then disappeared again. After another fairly long absence she returned and took our order, but by the time we finished eating we were already late for the evening session.

The return trip to the church was uneventful. When we arrived at the church, I locked the car, but said to Alice and our kids, "I'm locking the car but I'm not going to worry about it this time." The evening session was just as exciting as the morning and afternoon sessions, and finally it was time to head back to the motel. This time when we arrived at the car we found it locked! *"Submit yourselves, then, to God. Resist the devil and he will flee from you."* (James 4:7) *"When the devil had finished all this tempting, he left Him until an opportune time."* (Luke 4:13)

We arrived at the motel that night to find that power had been restored to all sections. We could have asked for a room with a working door lock, but decided to stay where we were for the rest of the weekend.

After a good breakfast in the morning, we arrived at the church early for the first time. We chose seats in the first row and before long one of the leaders came forward and said, "Is there anyone here who has experience operating a video camera?" My hand shot up immediately. He then pointed to me and said, "Your hand was up first. Would you come with me?" I followed him to the rear of the sanctuary where I was introduced to the director of the video crew. He explained that one cameraman could not be there that day so he needed someone to operate one of the cameras. He was pleased to hear that I had TV studio experience (even though it was 27 years ago), but wanted to test my skill before putting me to work. The director led me to the camera in the very rear corner of the auditorium, explained a few things about the camera, told me to put the headphones on, and then he returned to the control booth.

Soon he spoke to me through headphones, asking me to zoom in, zoom out, pan left, pan right, pan while zooming out and pan while zooming in. After accomplishing all of these tasks, he said, "I want you on the number one camera, down front." I said, "Are you sure?" He said, "Yes, you are the best cameraman I have today, and I want you on the main camera." I couldn't believe what I was hearing. I hadn't operated a studio camera in almost thirty years, and I'm the best they've got? Well, all I could think was, "Praise the Lord who heard my thoughts and fulfilled my wish!" *"Delight yourself in the Lord, and He will give you the desires of your heart."* (Psalm 37:4)

Operating a camera in such an environment is a mixed blessing. Beside the fact that I was on my feet for three sessions of at least four hours each, it was extremely difficult to keep my mind detached from what was going on in front of me. I heard testimonies from people whose lives had been changed. I heard stories of miraculous healings from the very people who had been healed. It was all I could do to keep from crying, and the director wanted really close "head and shoulders" shots, which is not an easy thing to do when the speaker moves around a lot. The camera action required my full attention. Although somewhat stressful, I still praise God for the opportunity to operate the big camera. About a month later I received two videotapes in the mail. They contained Saturday's video. Blessing upon blessing!

Sunday was the weekend's climax. A healing service in a local arena was scheduled for the afternoon, so we were on our own for breakfast and to attend a local church. Our group of eight decided to eat breakfast at the motel restaurant to save time and then attend a small storefront church that we had been invited to by the pastor.

On Sunday morning my family drove to our friends' rooms but found only one couple up and ready to go. It took a few knocks on the second door to awaken the other two, who had not received their wake–up call. We told our sleepy friend that we would wait for them to get ready, but she told us to go ahead and they would walk to the restaurant, which was just a short distance across the parking lot from their room. All six of us heard what she had said.

I drove my family the short distance to the restaurant, while the two friends who were ready, walked. Once all six of us were there, we requested a table for eight and were seated. We waited for what seemed to be an inordinate amount of time. When the other two finally entered the restaurant, they glanced in our direction and then sat on the opposite side of the restaurant. We were shocked. They didn't look happy at all. Alice said, "I'm going over there to find out why they're not sitting with us." We all watched with interest, and although we could tell a heated discussion was going on, we couldn't hear what was being said and that made us even more curious. Finally, they got up and came to our table with Alice. Once seated with us, they *insisted* that they had said, "Wait for us, we'll get ready quickly and be right with you." They were angry because we didn't wait for them. We had a difficult time convincing them of what the six of us had heard, but we all finally agreed that Satan was trying to divide us and distract us from our mission for the day.

After breakfast, we attended the storefront worship service, ate lunch, and finally arrived at the arena for the afternoon service. The leaders divided everyone into healing teams and gave each person a ribbon to identify them as such. After an opening prayer, Frances placed her hand on the head of each person as she walked down the line of healing team members, anointing each person. Most of the people fell under the power of the Holy Spirit, caught by the person standing behind them for this purpose. It was a moving experience. When Frances placed her hand on my head, I felt my entire body relax and my knees begin to bend. I just went limp. It was the most relaxing and peaceful feeling I had ever experienced. I didn't fall over but I swayed and took a half step backward. I felt the hands of the catcher behind me steadying me. After the anointing we went to our assigned locations for the healing service.

I have long since forgotten the details of that afternoon, save a couple of experiences. Before the main event began and only the healing team, pastors, family and friends were present, we enjoyed a short praise service. Many of the people were singing in tongues and the magnificent sound in that large arena was like nothing I had ever heard before or since. It was truly amazing. I suppose heaven must sound a lot like the arena that day.

I know firsthand that many were healed that day. One healing that sticks in my mind was an elderly man with two hearing aids. He had difficulty hearing us when we asked him what he needed. He wanted his hearing restored. I asked him to remove both hearing aids. I then tried to tell him what I was going to do but he couldn't hear me at all. So, I simply stuck my fingers in his ears, commanded the ears to open and allow hearing to be restored in Jesus' name. As I pulled my fingers from his ears he fell backward into the hands of the catcher who lowered him gently onto the floor. When he got up, he could hear everything we said in a normal voice. Hallelujah!

Satan's Grip

"Be self–controlled and alert. Your enemy the devil prowls around like a roaring lion looking for someone to devour." (1 Peter 5:8)

Little did Alice and I know that through our trip to Allentown, Pennsylvania, God was preparing us for a battle. Not a battle of our own, but as soldiers of God to stand in the breach for a friend. God allowed us to learn the truth about the presence of angels—both heavenly and demonic—and the spiritual and physical power they can assert. Without this experience and knowledge, I'm not sure our friend's life and the lives of his family would have been saved. This is the story of our friend Mark and his struggle with Satan.

Mark grew up as I did, enjoying everything electronic and/or technical. Ham radio, radio controlled airplanes and boats, and other fascinating hobbies were a natural for us both. I knew Mark and his wife from church, but our friendship grew as we found our interests paralleled so closely.

This part of the story is how we differed. When the Lord fully awakened me to His presence, I accepted Him anew. I was "born again." I was excited, began to grow in faith by leaps and bounds, and experienced miracles! God got Mark's attention as well and one warm summer Sunday as our Sunday school class was meeting at a church member's farm, Mark accepted the Lord by his confession to the group. Mark however, had a different reaction to his being "born again." Satan was NOT happy!

Mark had been diagnosed with bipolar disorder, which I was not aware of at the time. His condition was being treated with Lithium and his mood swings seemed to be pretty well controlled. When Mark accepted the Lord, you might say "all hell broke loose!" Mark's depression grew to new lows, and he became suicidal and homicidal. Mark was now hearing voices that told him to kill his family and then himself.

Mark and his wife began to call Alice and I and plead for us to come and pray for them. Many times these calls came at two or three o'clock in the morning. This did not sit well with me, having to get up early to go to my job! But, we were obedient. (We were not happy about it, but obedient none–the–less.)

The first thing we did was to rid Mark's house of a shotgun and ammunition. Then we prayed. Often Alice and I would simply quote Scripture and Mark would relax. (Satan hates to hear Scripture!) (Remember when David played music and the evil spirit in Saul would give him a little peace?) This went on for some time. Mark even spent some time in the psychiatric wing of the local hospital. All the hospital could do was medicate him however, and this did not address the real need.

On several occasions Alice and I commanded the demons to leave. Since we were fairly new at this deliverance stuff, we weren't so sure of ourselves. I'm sure the demons laughed at our feeble attempts, at least for a while. We did not give up though, and one night in particular remains vivid in my memory. Mark and his wife sat next to each other on the couch and Alice and I began commanding the demons to come out of one and then the other. Once when I commanded the demons to come out of Mark in the name of Jesus, the lamp next to him went completely dark and then light again. That was the only light affected even though we had all the lights on in two adjacent rooms. It seemed as though darkness itself had passed through the lamp!

As I cast out demons in Mark, his wife's head would fall back as though someone had pushed on her forehead, and her mouth was held wide open. When I turned to Mark's wife and commanded the demons to come out, she relaxed, but Mark's head would go back and his mouth opened wide. I began to realize that the demons were playing with us. Finally we ordered the demons not to reenter the person. I was amazed that demons could control humans like this, but it certainly made the Bible stories all the more real! But God triumphed! Through our obedience and persistence, and God's power, Mark was delivered from the demons that tormented both him and his family, and Mark has grown as a Christian, even obtaining a Master of Divinity degree.

Never underestimate the power of evil, but trust in the power of God! *"When they came to Jesus, they saw the man who had been possessed by the legion of demons, sitting there, dressed and in his right mind; and they were afraid."* (Mark 5:15) *"Heal the sick, raise the dead, cleanse those who have leprosy, drive out demons. Freely you have received, freely give."* (Matthew 10:8) *"The seventy–two returned with joy and said, 'Lord, even the demons submit to us in your name.' He replied, 'I saw Satan fall like lightning from heaven.'"* (Luke 10:17–18)

Chapter III: Miracles

Donald

The workplace can be a hostile environment for Christians, but now and then you find a scattered few who are willing to pursue a study of God's Word before work or at lunch time. I had a few opportunities to join groups in various work locations after my healing experiences, and often, healing became the subject of our discussion. (God's miracles cannot be kept in the dark!)

Donald was a coworker in one of those Bible studies, and he had a big problem for a young man. He was diagnosed with osteoporosis at the age of only 28 years old! After hearing about some of my healing experiences in our Bible group, he came to my office one day while I was eating my lunch. He explained his problems to me and said that he was in terrible pain, which was obvious by the way he walked—bent over, slowly and deliberately. Osteoporosis was causing his bones to shrink and lose density, thereby allowing pinching and rubbing of nerves and tissue that would normally be protected by the bones. Donald said he had been given experimental medicine to increase bone mass, but because his body chemistry was different than those for whom the medicine was developed (as he put it, "Little old ladies"), the medicine had no effect on him. He was also put on an experimental program that NASA had developed to help astronauts maintain bone mass. He was bouncing on a trampoline! According to Donald (and NASA), it is the jolts or bounces that produce greater bone mass—except in Donald. His bone mass was still on a steady decline. He had even been given steroids for 18 months. Nothing had helped.

With Donald facing me, I bound the spirit of osteoporosis and commanded that spirit to come out of him. Then I bound the spirit of pain and commanded that spirit to come out of him. I commanded the bone mass to stop decreasing and to increase and return to normal. Each time something was commanded or a spirit bound, it was done in the name of Jesus. Donald began to sway slightly and headed for a nearby chair. He said his knees and legs suddenly got weak. I told him that was the Holy Spirit working on him! After a few minutes of sitting, Donald stood up STRAIGHT and WITHOUT PAIN, and left my office (still somewhat wobbly).

Over the next weeks and months I kept in touch with Donald and discovered that not only was his pain gone, but his doctor informed him that his pituitary gland began working again. I didn't know his pituitary gland hadn't been working, but God healed it anyway. The doctor told Donald, "Once a pituitary gland stops working, it is medically impossible to make it work again." But, she had to admit that something had happened.

A month or so later Donald went back to the doctor for a follow–up bone scan. A few days after the scan, just as Donald was about to listen to a voicemail message from his doctor, Donald's wife called saying she "felt in her heart" that she needed to call him at that moment. So, they listened to the doctor's report together. (August 18, 1992) The doctor stated that while she expected 20% to 30% bone loss, THERE WAS NO EVIDENCE OF OSTEOPOROSIS! Also, the doctor stated there is no way medicine could cause this to happen! *"For you are great and do marvelous deeds; you alone are God."* (Psalms 86:10)

Thomas

This Thomas was no "doubting Thomas." Once again, but in a different location, I attended a Bible study at my place of work. I told the group about the healing power of God in my life and some of the amazing stories concerning others who have been healed, including Donald's story. Although they seemed to be interested,

I couldn't tell if they really believed me. Thomas was among those attending the Bible study.

One day while sitting at my desk eating a late lunch and relaxing, Thomas entered my office. He told me he believed in healing and had heard what I said. He said his wife had been suffering with stomach pain for a few months. Although she had been to three doctors, they could find nothing wrong with her. Could I pray for her?

Certainly I could pray for her. With Thomas standing next to me and with me still seated, I simply reached up and placed my hand on Thomas' stomach and said, "In the name of Jesus, I command this man's wife's stomach to be healed!" I didn't even know her name. We both said "Thank you Jesus," then Thomas thanked me and returned to his office. I returned my attention to my lunch.

The next morning Thomas came to my office and said, "I have to tell you what happened when I got home last night. I had forgotten about praying for my wife, but when I got to the door my wife met me and said; 'The strangest thing happened about one o'clock this afternoon. I had this warm feeling in my stomach and the pain left. I haven't had any pain in my stomach the rest of the day!'" I said "WOW! That's the very time we prayed for her!"

"Then Jesus said to the centurion, 'Go! It will be done just as you believed it would.' And his servant was healed at that very hour." (Matthew 8:13)

Parking Lot Attendant

At the time of my fasting and the above healing, I worked in a building with a parking garage (connected by a bridge/breezeway), which normally charged for parking. Our company obtained parking passes for all of the employees which allowed us to park for free, but we still had to pass the attendant and wait for the "gate" to open (a single bar across the entrance).

The parking lot attendant was a very pleasant man in his fifties, from Nicaragua. I would often park my car and then walk back out the entrance at street level so I could talk to the attendant and learn something about him. Although there wasn't a lot of time to talk, I did learn that he was a dentist in his home country but couldn't get certification in the United States, and he would have to start over with his education to do so. So he was a parking garage attendant to support his wife. I don't remember now about his children, but he did mention he had a mother and sister, still in Nicaragua. This man was forced to leave his country because of the civil unrest which put men in great danger, especially well educated men with good jobs.

One morning as I entered the garage, he told me that his mother was dying of cancer. I could tell his eyes were tearing up, but I couldn't stop and talk just then, so I decided to come back when we both had more time.

That day at lunch time I walked to his post at the entrance of the parking garage, and after getting some details from him, I prayed with him, commanding the spirit of Cancer in his mother to be bound and cast out. I commanded any damage to her body caused by the cancer to be healed, and I commanded a new immune system to come into her body to fight any attempts of the cancer to come back or remain. I cursed the seed, root and cell of the cancer growth and commanded it to die. All of this was commanded in the name of Jesus.

I kept checking with him to find out how she was doing, and finally he had heard from his sister, and she said their mother had been HEALED! Praise the LORD!

Over the following months I would talk with the (now excited) parking lot attendant, and he would relate to me how well his mother was doing.

But then one day I came to work and I could tell as I approached the parking garage that the attendant wanted to talk and his face was downcast. I asked him what was wrong and he said his mother had died. I blurted out, "But I thought she was healed!" "Oh" he said, "She was. She was healed of the cancer and that's why my mother and sister went to Mexico. She was doing so well that they decided to take a vacation and go to Mexico, and she died there of a heart attack."

Lazarus was brought back from death by Jesus. But where is he now? Sometimes it's hard to remember that the mortality rate of humans is 100%. Even when we're healed of some malady, death still comes at some time. Healing then is not for immortality, but for opening our eyes (and hearts and minds) to God's possibilities. ALL things are possible with God. That also means that nothing is impossible for God!

"Jesus rebuked the demon, and it came out of the boy, and he was healed from that moment. Then the disciples came to Jesus in private and asked, 'Why couldn't we drive it out?' He replied, 'Because you have so little faith. I tell you the truth, if you have faith as small as a mustard seed, you can say to this mountain, Move from here to there and it will move. Nothing will be impossible for you.'" (Matthew 17:18–20)

Thyroid

Sometime prior to 1993 I began fasting. Fasting can take many forms. We learn from the book of Daniel that, *"I ate no choice food; no meat or wine touched my lips; and I used no lotions at all until the three weeks were over."* (Daniel 10:3). Another fast included neither eating nor drinking for three days. (Esther 4:16) Another type of fasting has nothing to do with denying oneself, except in service to others: *"Is this the kind of fast I have chosen, only a day for a man to humble himself? Is it only for bowing one's head like a reed and for lying on sackcloth and ashes? Is that what you call a fast, a day acceptable to the LORD? Is not this the kind of fasting I have chosen: to loose the chains of injustice and untie the cords of the yoke, to set the oppressed free and break every yoke? Is it not to share your food with the hungry and to provide the poor wanderer with shelter—when you see the naked, to clothe him, and not to turn away from your own flesh and blood? Then your light will break forth like the dawn, and your healing will quickly appear; then your righteousness will go before you, and the glory of the LORD will be your rear guard. Then you will call, and the LORD will answer; you will cry for help, and he will say: Here am I. If you do away with the yoke of oppression, with the pointing finger and malicious talk, and if you spend yourselves in behalf of the hungry and satisfy the needs of the oppressed, then your light will rise in the darkness, and your night will become like the noonday. The LORD will guide you always; he will satisfy your needs in a sun–scorched land and will strengthen your frame. You will be like a well–watered garden, like a spring whose waters never fail."* (Isaiah 58:5–11) God is more interested in our heart than our stomach.

After reading Scriptures and a few books about fasting, I decided that my fast would consist of: No breakfast or lunch on one day of the week. A day in the book of Genesis (and in the Middle East even today) is evening and morning, so the day begins and ends at sundown. I figured suppertime–to–suppertime was close enough.

People often ask, "Why fast?" Jesus mentioned fasting as though it were a way of life, not an oddity. (In Matthew 6:16 for instance, Jesus says, *"When you fast...."*) I believe there is spiritual power in prayer and *fasting.* Only after fasting can you answer the question, "Why fast?" I discovered that fasting made me think about God often. Every time I was hungry I thought about God, then said a prayer for someone or praised God. The purpose of fasting is, after all, to help us draw nearer to God.

After several months of fasting one day a week, I decided to fast two days a week. This is not an easy thing to do—especially in the workplace—as everyone around you seems to have a mission to get you to eat. Fasting is also complicated by impromptu group lunches, birthday celebrations, and other company functions. Still, once my coworkers got over the novelty of my fasting I continued without interference. There *is* power in fasting and prayer! I also discovered that I wasn't nearly as hungry.

I had been fasting for about a year and a half when I noticed a red rash on both sides of my chin, from my cheeks down both sides of my neck. The rash didn't last long so I never went to the doctor to find out what it was.

Shortly after the rash disappeared, I began losing weight and suffered from severe colds. My weight eventually dropped from 180 Lbs to 134 Lbs. Just as I would recover from one cold, another one would flare up. I became very weak, struggling even to walk. Every exertion made my heart pound. Some nights my heart pounded so hard it caused the bed to shake with every beat. I wasn't sleeping well and I was afraid I was keeping Alice awake as well.

I finally went to the doctor to get something for my unshakable cold. While there, the doctor took a blood test.

I received a call at work a few days later from my doctor, saying he wanted to see me. I said, "Ok, I'll make an appointment in a day or so." He said, "No, I want you to come in RIGHT NOW!" I took the afternoon off and drove directly to the doctor's office.

The doctor informed me that my problem was a hyperactive thyroid and gave me a prescription for anti–thyroid pills, which I was to begin taking immediately. Do not pass go, do not collect $200, go directly to the pharmacy and get this prescription filled! He also referred me to an endocrinologist. I told the doctor that I wasn't concerned because God would heal me. He told me not to get my hopes up, as thyroid problems do not go away. I said "I don't accept that in the name of Jesus. God will heal me."

The next day I got the prescription filled (I didn't listen to the doctor about getting it filled immediately) and made an appointment with the specialist. I also ended my fasting at my doctor's recommendation.

The specialist scheduled a sonogram to determine the extent of the thyroid problem. She said it was enlarged but needed a more specific measurement. She also wrote a new prescription, doubling the amount of anti–thyroid medicine that my doctor had prescribed. The result of the sonogram showed that my thyroid was approximately 10% enlarged. My options, according to the specialist, were: an operation to physically remove some of the thyroid, radiation to kill part of the thyroid, or to continue taking the anti–thyroid medication for the rest of my life. I told the specialist that I would be healed and I would take the pills for the time being. She said, "Don't get your hopes up. Only about 10% of people with thyroid problems are ever healed." I said, "I will be one of those 10%."

I took the anti–thyroid pills from May through December 1993, and haven't taken one since. My weight returned to normal and my health was restored. I have had no problem with my thyroid since then. God did heal me. I haven't fasted since then, but I learned quite a bit from the experience.

Words of doubt

Mom was the church person in our family. Mom was involved in the church and always made sure my brother and I were in attendance weekly, including Sunday school and Youth Group. Dad on the other hand would rather go fishing. Still, he came occasionally and even made sure we got to church even if Mom couldn't.

When Alice and I got really excited about the Lord and all that was going on, I told my parents all about it. Dad's comment was, "Religion is fine, but don't get too involved." Well, we did get involved, and eventually, both Mom and Dad accepted the Lord, perhaps for the first time or just renewed, but they accepted the Lord. *"...and a little child shall lead them."* (Isaiah 11:6) Well, I wasn't a little child, but I was *their* child and I was privileged to be able to lead them to the Lord.

Dad had worn two hearing aids for several years, no doubt from all the hammering (he was a carpenter) and shooting high powered rifles (he enjoyed hunting and shooting) for many years. Alice and I were living in Maryland at the time, and my parents were still living in Pennsylvania, so we didn't see each other all that often, maybe once or twice a month. On one of our visits, I thought we might as well see if the Lord would restore Dad's hearing. Dad, Alice and I (and our kids) were in the living room, and Mom was in the kitchen, around the corner through a doorway, behind dad. With me facing Dad and Alice behind him, I had him remove his hearing aids and then explained what I was going to do, but he couldn't hear me very well. I had to raise my voice and finally he understood. I placed my fingers in his ears. I bound the spirit of deafness and commanded his hearing to be restored in the name of Jesus. I removed my fingers from his ears. I asked him in a soft voice if he could hear me. He said, "Yes, I hear you." Then Alice asked him if he could hear her (she was still behind him), and he said, "yes, I can hear you." Then we asked Mom to say something to him, which she did, and he could even hear her from the other room! For the rest of the day we could hold a normal conversation. No one had to raise their voice! Dad didn't need his hearing aids!

I was excited on our next trip to visit my parents, and see how Dad was doing without his hearing aids. To my shock and surprise, he was wearing his hearing aids again! I asked him why he was wearing his hearing aids, and he said, "I'm old, and you know when you get old, your hearing goes and you can't hear very well. I need my hearing aids."

Alice and I did exactly what we had done before. I once again commanded healing in Jesus name, and once again, we spent the rest of the day holding normal conversations—without Dad wearing his hearing aids. I told him that he does not need his hearing aids and he needs to rebuke the devil when he thinks he does need them. After explaining what "rebuke" means, Alice and I and our children headed for Maryland.

On our next trip to Pennsylvania, I was again filled with joy to think that Dad didn't need his hearing aids any longer. But once again, as we entered the house, I noticed Dad wearing his hearing aids again. I practically shouted, "Why are you wearing your hearing aids?" Dad said, "Well, I'm an old man, and when you get old, your hearing doesn't work very well, so I need my hearing aids." I was not happy, but what could I do.

This story reminds me that when the angel Gabriel visited Zechariah to tell him about Elizabeth having a baby (John, who became the "Baptist"), the angel had to shut Zechariah's mouth until after John was born because Zechariah was speaking doubt and disbelief! (Luke 1)

But in contrast, when Gabriel visited Mary to tell her that she would bear a son, Mary said, "may it be to me as you have said!" Sure she wondered "how can this be?" but she didn't speak negative words! We can actually destroy God's plans with our words! It's hard to believe that there are people who do not want to be healed, but there are!

During our trip to Allentown, Pennsylvania with the Hunter Healing team, I prayed for a man in a wheelchair, and he made absolutely no effort to get out of that chair. He just sat there and looked at me, then explained that he had been prayed for before and nothing happened. He didn't expect anything to happen, and

I don't think he wanted anything to happen. And, he was a former pastor! Knowing the Word of God doesn't give us faith, only living the Word of God and trusting that Word gives us faith. How many people miss a miracle because they are afraid it will change their lifestyle?

No wonder Jesus asked the people, *"Do you want to get well?"* (John 5:6), and *"'What do you want me to do for you?' 'Lord, I want to see,' he replied. Jesus said to him, 'Receive your sight; your faith has healed you.'"* (Luke 18:41–42)

After the second time of healing my dad's hearing, I never brought up the subject again. At age 95, Dad is still wearing his hearing aids, and even with them, the conversation has to be loud to be heard.

Chapter IV: God's Word

New Direction

God has changed our direction a bit over the years since those first exciting days of seeing the Holy Spirit at work in our lives and in the lives around us. Oh, we have been aware of the Holy Spirit at work, but the laying on of hands and prayer for healing slacked off, and we entered a more "mainstream" part of the ministry. Alice received an undeniable call into the ministry and now serves the Lord as pastor of a church. We have taught the healing class a few times, but most teaching now is Bible study related, such as the excellent "Disciple" program.

Although I often said I would never teach or preach, God just laughs at our feeble attempts to resist Him, and I began teaching AND preaching. God amazingly has given me whole sermons while brushing my teeth, showering and getting dressed. Scriptures often flood through my head (remember all those times of listening to the Bible? God had to get His Word into my head and heart so he could bring it to my mind later!) So Alice and I both minister in ways we would never have dreamed about, but we wouldn't have it any other way. To serve the Lord is our JOY!

Recently, we have felt the moving of God's Spirit in that direction once more. Perhaps the time is right for another display of God's power. Both Alice and I have been privileged to see people healed miraculously as the command is spoken in the name of Jesus. For instance, one evening during a Bible study, one young mother was telling me that she has been having terrible pain in her hip and couldn't even hold her young daughter for more than a few minutes. I explained to her a little about how we "pray" for people, and asked her if she was willing. She said she was, so I had her remain seated, and face me. I sat in a chair facing her, and placing my hands on her ankles with my thumbs on her ankle bones, I lifted her feet until her legs were about level with the floor. By putting my thumbs close together, I could tell that one leg was "longer" than the other (a sign that the hips were not in alignment). I then commanded the hips to go into alignment, the vertebrae, disks, muscles, tendons, ligaments, and nerves to go into proper alignment and to stay that way. I also commanded the muscles to be strengthened and to hold the back and hips in their proper position. All of this I asked in the name of Jesus. I then had her say, "Thank you Jesus." I had her stand up and twist and bend to see if the pain was gone. She stood and twisted one way and we all heard two loud "pops." Then she twisted the other way and we heard one even louder "POP." She bent over and when she stood up again, she had a funny smile on her face. I asked her if she had any pain, and she said, "NO!" She also told me that when she sits for a short while, she has trouble standing, but she practically jumped up when I told her to stand.

Now that she was healed, she told me about her daughter. Something was wrong with her young daughter's platelets and she had never slept through the night, usually waking early in the morning and wanting to be held. So, I put my hand on this young mother's shoulder and commanded her daughter's platelets to be normal, the blood to be purified and whole, and the chemical balance in her body to be normal. Again, I commanded all of this in the name of Jesus.

The following Sunday this young mother told me that her daughter had slept through that night until 7 a.m., took a nap that afternoon (which she had not done before), and had been sleeping "normally" ever since our prayer. Praise the LORD!

Healing isn't done necessarily for the healing alone, and this situation is a good example. The husband of this young mother wasn't interested in church, but after the healing of his daughter, he became interested and began attending the worship service. God got his attention and turned his thoughts to Him!

Our Dash

"Where can I go from your Spirit? Where can I flee from your presence? If I go up to the heavens, you are there; if I make my bed in the depths, you are there. If I rise on the wings of the dawn, if I settle on the far side of the sea, even there your hand will guide me, your right hand will hold me fast. If I say, 'Surely the darkness will hide me and the light become night around me,' even the darkness will not be dark to you; the night will shine like the day, for darkness is as light to you. For you created my inmost being; you knit me together in my mother's womb. I praise you because I am fearfully and wonderfully made; your works are wonderful, I know that full well." (Psalm 139:7–14)

God has wooed me and won. No matter how often I stray from the narrow path, I know that He forgives me and loves me. I am His and will serve Him imperfectly until the day I go to meet Him.

I am now doing all the things I once said I would never do, like teaching and preaching. It really is a joy to serve the Lord. Although Alice and I are now in the "mainstream" of the church we are anticipating an outpouring of God's Holy Spirit for exciting miracles. We still see God at work all around us, but not as excitingly as in the recent past. It's all in God's time and for His purpose. Meanwhile, we serve the Lord patiently.

The following is a sermon given by the author in November 2006.

What will you do with your "DASH?" Will you make a difference or will you move on into obscurity with no affect on the kingdom of God? What is your dash? Do you think of it as your handsome or beautiful looks, a pleasant demeanor, or charisma? Well, I'm talking about a different dash.

I know you have all seen a grave marker. What information is on the marker in most cases? Name, Date Born, and Deceased Date. In our case (I assume we are all still breathing, but you might want to check with your neighbor), we have only the Name and Date Born so far.

So what does this have to do with our DASH? The DASH is the most important thing on the grave marker. It separates the date born from the date deceased. It is the time between our birth and death. On the grave marker it says the least, but encompasses everything we have ever done, or in our case, everything we *will* do as well. Our "dash" is our entire life.

Paul said in Hebrews 3:7–8 *"So, as the Holy Spirit says: 'Today, if you hear His voice, do not harden your hearts....'"* Since you and I still have a "today," we need to follow the Lord, and if we haven't fully accepted Him, we need to do that...before they put that last date on some marble or granite for us. Jesus said in John 9:4 *"As long as it is day, we must do the work of him who sent me. Night is coming, when no one can work. Work while it is day. Night is coming when no one can work."* Day is our "dash" and night is after the second date is put on our stone.

Remember the Old Testament book about Ruth? Ruth was living in an idol worshipping country, but had married a young Hebrew from Bethlehem. Even though her husband died shortly thereafter, Ruth chose to follow her mother–in–law and move to Israel, caring for her mother–in–law and honoring the God of the Israelites. She made a good decision. Through her "good decisions" and love and support of her mother–in–law, she ended up marrying an honorable man (who just happened to be well–off), and bearing the grandfather of King David. Do you understand the importance of the story? We don't know what ever happened to the other daughter–in–law of Naomi, as we never hear about her again. Perhaps her "dash" ended up in obscurity. At least she got an "honorable mention" in the Scripture, but Ruth is the hero. She changed lives and brought praise for her mother–in–law. Honoring God and making good decisions makes a difference.

Jesus said the teachers of the law could have used their lives in a better way. They were puffed up. Instead of making a difference in other people's lives in a positive way, they enjoyed their place of honor and taught others to be like them.

In the Temple as people came to put money into the treasury, Jesus commented on the difference between the rich people and the widow. Those who had wealth gave impressive amounts, but pittance by comparison to what they had. In contrast, the widow didn't have much to give, but she gave *all she had*! She made a right decision to honor God and give whatever she had. We don't have any "follow–up" on the rich people or the poor widow, but we know that God is the rewarder of those who honor Him so we can imagine the outcome. Jesus had much to say about the rich people not because of there wealth, but because of what they did (or didn't do) with it. Consider the story of the rich man and Lazarus.

What about other examples of people using their lives to make a difference in the lives of others? One of my favorite stories is about Joseph. Mistreated by his brothers, he was thrown into a pit and then sold to a caravan of Ishmaelites heading for Egypt. They in turn sold Joseph as a slave to Potiphar, one of Pharaoh's officials and Captain of the guard. What did Joseph do? Did he moan and complain and refuse to do more than absolutely necessary? NO! Joseph did the best he could, honoring God and his master Potiphar. Genesis 39:2–6 tells us: *"The LORD was with Joseph and he prospered, and he lived in the house of his Egyptian master. When his master saw that the LORD was with him and that the LORD gave him success in everything he did, Joseph found favor in his eyes and became his attendant. Potiphar put him in charge of his household, and he entrusted to his care everything he owned. From the time he put him in charge of his household and of all that he owned, the LORD blessed the household of the Egyptian because of Joseph. The blessing of the LORD was on everything Potiphar had, both in the house and in the field. So he left in Joseph's care everything he had; with Joseph in charge, he did not concern himself with anything except the food he ate."*

Sounds good so far, but the story doesn't end here. Joseph's "dash" continues. Potiphar's wife had a desire for Joseph and when he refused her advances, she falsely accused him of trying to rape her. Joseph is thrown in jail.

Did Joseph mope around and moan about how life is unfair? NO! Genesis 39:20–23 tells us: *"Joseph's master took him and put him in prison, the place where the king's prisoners were confined. But while Joseph was there in the prison, the LORD was with him; He showed him kindness and granted him favor in the eyes of the prison warden. the warden put Joseph in charge of all those held in the prison, and he was made responsible for all that was done there. The warden paid no attention to anything under Joseph's care, because the LORD was with Joseph and gave him success in whatever he did."* Joseph continued to honor God with right decisions and doing the best with whatever opportunity he had to serve.

Joseph thought he might get out of his predicament when he was given an interpretation to the dreams of Pharaoh's cup bearer and Pharaoh's baker. He tells the cup bearer to put in a good word for him when he (the cup bearer) is restored to his former position, but two full years pass and nothing happens. Joseph might have given up, but he trusted in God. Everything happens in God's time. Finally, Pharaoh has a dream and the cup bearer remembers his experience with Joseph. The story ends well and Joseph ends up as the number two man in Egypt. Except for matters of the throne itself, Joseph is in charge of Egypt. Most people would end the story here. After all, it is a good story. Joseph always did the right thing, no matter what the circumstances. He trusted God no matter what the situation. But that's not the end of the story. God has one more scene for Joseph to play out.

Joseph's brothers come to Egypt to buy food. Joseph knows who *they* are, but they don't recognize him. (Joseph was about 17 when he was sold into slavery, and he is now about 34!) After some deceit and trickery on Joseph's part, he forgives his brothers for their actions. Genesis 45:4–8 *"Then Joseph said to his brothers, 'Come close to me.' When they had done so, he said, 'I am your brother Joseph, the one you sold into Egypt! And now, do not be distressed and do not be angry with yourselves for selling me here, because it was to save lives that God sent me ahead of you. For two years now there has been famine in the land, and for the next five years there will not be plowing and reaping. But God sent me ahead of you to preserve for you a remnant on earth and to save your lives by a great deliverance. So then, it was not you who sent me here, but God. He made me father to Pharaoh, lord of his entire household and ruler of all Egypt.'"*

When we look at a grave marker we have no idea what that "dash" represents, unless we knew the person, or know what that person had done. Sometimes the name gives us information about the person's life. For instance: Jesus, Paul, Elijah, Samson, Noah, and even some non–Biblical persons: Jonas Salk, George Washington, Abraham Lincoln, and John Wesley. I'm not saying we need to be famous to have a worthwhile life. Quite the contrary. I want *MY* name to be written in the Lamb's Book of Life! That's my goal. I also want to help as many people as possible get *their* names written in the Lamb's Book of Life. People may look at my "dash" and wonder what it represents, but God will know, and He's the One I care about.

What will you do with your "dash?" Will you put something worthwhile between those two dates? Paul said in Philippians 3:5–8 (I was) *"circumcised on the eighth day, of the people of Israel, of the tribe of Benjamin, a Hebrew of Hebrews; in regard to the law, a Pharisee; as for zeal, persecuting the church; as for legalistic righteousness, faultless. But whatever was to my profit I now consider loss for the sake of Christ. What is more, I consider everything a loss compared to the surpassing greatness of knowing Christ Jesus my Lord, for whose sake I have lost all things. I consider them rubbish, that I may gain Christ."* In other words, credentials and pedigree don't mean a thing if you don't have Jesus in your life. If you aren't doing what is pleasing to God, you are wasting your life.

Of course our best example of how to live our lives comes from Jesus. Understanding how Jesus wants us to live is a life–long study. As we learn more we can pass on more and help others understand. How are you serving the Lord so that you will make a contribution to the future?

I know a Muslim man who was touched by the willingness of a Christian neighbor to help dig a garden. Perhaps God will water that seed elsewhere and bring that man to salvation. I know another person who was so touched by the willingness of a Christian neighbor to cut some weeds that he made a dramatic change in his life. Are you willing to be used by God? We don't have to do great things. We need to simply be willing to be used by God in whatever situation we find ourselves.

May the God of the universe mold us into willing vessels and pour into us His love, wisdom and knowledge, so abundantly that it will spill over onto everyone we meet. May we be filled with His Holy Spirit and with power to teach and preach and lead others to the *way*, the *truth*, and the *life*. Let us build up the Kingdom of God! Let us make our "DASH" worthwhile! Amen.

Don't Go Fishing

The following sermon was given by the author in January, 2009.

"Then the word of the LORD came to Jonah a second time:

'Go to the great city of Nineveh and proclaim to it the message I give you.' Jonah obeyed the word of the LORD and went to Nineveh. Now Nineveh was a very important city—a visit required three days. On the first day, Jonah started into the city. He proclaimed: 'Forty more days and Nineveh will be overturned.' The Ninevites believed God. They declared a fast, and all of them, from the greatest to the least, put on sackcloth. When God saw what they did and how they turned from their evil ways, he had compassion and did not bring upon them the destruction he had threatened." (Jonah 3:1–5, 10)

"When I say to a wicked man, 'You will surely die,' and you do not warn him or speak out to dissuade him from his evil ways in order to save his life, that wicked man will die for his sin, and I will hold you accountable for his blood. But if you do warn the wicked man and he does not turn from his wickedness or from his evil ways, he will die for his sin; but you will have saved yourself. Again, when a righteous man turns from his righteousness and does evil, and I put a stumbling block before him, he will die. Since you did not warn him, he will die for his sin. The righteous things he did will not be remembered, and I will hold you accountable for his blood. But if you do warn the righteous man not to sin and he does not sin, he will surely live because he took warning, and you will have saved yourself." (Ezekiel 3:18–21)

This sermon is about being called. You just heard how Jonah was told a second time to go to Nineveh. Now I want to talk about Moses being called. We all know the story of the Israelites coming

Egypt and all the miracles that God performed, but let's look ne story of God CALLING Moses.

Moses was tending his father–in–law's sheep "in the back of the desert." This is probably a comment meaning "away from everything" or "really remote!" Moses is drawn to that famous burning bush that is not consumed by the fire, and it turns out to be "the angel of the Lord." (Or God Himself!) Anyway, after a few pleasantries and to get Moses into the right frame of mind for Worship (Take off your shoes...), God speaks to Moses through the burning bush. Basically, God says He has heard the plight of the Israelites and has decided to help them. So, the Lord God wants Moses to go to Egypt and tell Pharaoh to let the Israelites go. Now picture this; Moses is prostrate, hearing the voice of God, in front of a burning bush that seems to be like the fake logs in a gas fireplace. You would expect Moses to say "Yes Sir! Right away Sir!" But what does Moses say? *"But Moses said to God, 'Who am I that I should go to Pharaoh, and that I should bring the children of Israel out of Egypt?'"* (Exodus 3:11)

God reassures Moses by saying that He (God) will be with him. Good enough? No! Moses says, *"...Suppose I go to the Israelites and say to them, 'The God of your fathers has sent me to you,' and they ask me, 'What is His name?' Then what shall I tell them?"* (Exodus 3:13)

Now right about here, if this was a child of ours and we told them to do something, after two "buts" or "what–ifs," we'd be getting a wee bit short tempered.

God says, "I AM WHO I AM. Tell them 'I AM' has sent you." (Just so there's no confusion, God also tells Moses to tell the Israelites that the Lord God of Abraham, Isaac, and Jacob sent him – it's the SAME GOD)

There! That should do it. No more excuses. Well, not quite. *"Then Moses answered and said, 'But suppose they will not believe me or listen to my voice; suppose they say, The LORD has not appeared to you.'"* (Exodus 4:1) Ok, how many parents would still be speaking in that loving soft voice by now? Three strikes and you're out. Go to your room and come out when you decide to follow my orders!

The Lord (patient parent that He is) then shows Moses how use his staff to prove that God really did speak with him by turning it into a snake.

Ok, *NOW* are we done with the excuses? Hmmm... not quite. *"Then Moses said to the LORD, 'O my Lord, I am not eloquent, neither before nor since You have spoken to Your servant; but I am slow of speech and slow of tongue.'"* (Exodus 4:10)

That's the fourth excuse. But God comes right back. *"So the LORD said to him, 'Who has made man's mouth? Or who makes the mute, the deaf, the seeing, or the blind? Have not I, the LORD? Now therefore, go, and I will be with your mouth and teach you what you shall say.'"* (Exodus 4:11–12)

Moses has one final plea: *"But he said, 'O my Lord, please send by the hand of whomever else You may send.'"* (Exodus 4:13)

"So the anger of the LORD was kindled against Moses, and He said: 'Is not Aaron the Levite your brother? I know that he can speak well. And look, he is also coming out to meet you. When he sees you, he will be glad in his heart. Now you shall speak to him and put the words in his mouth. And I will be with your mouth and with his mouth, and I will teach you what you shall do. So he shall be your spokesman to the people. And he himself shall be as a mouth for you, and you shall be to him as God.'" (Exodus 4:14–16)

How many times do we anger the Lord when He calls us and we give excuses? This is an extraordinary story of God's persistence and man's excuses. But it happens every day. God calls and we give excuses. We might think if God called us in a dramatic way like the way He called Moses, we could be sure it was the Lord doing the asking. Do you really think that would make any difference? It isn't just the Israelites who are a stiff–necked people!

"'Before I formed you in the womb I knew you, before you were born I set you apart; I appointed you as a prophet to the nations.' 'Ah, Sovereign LORD,' I said, 'I do not know how to speak; I am only a child.'" (Jeremiah 1:5–6) God promises to teach his mouth to speak and also promises to be with him. God will not call us and send us without first preparing us!

When the angel of the LORD appeared to Gideon, he said, 'The RD is with you, mighty warrior.' 'But sir,' Gideon replied, 'if the ORD is with us, why has all this happened to us? Where are all His wonders that our fathers told us about when they said, "Did not the LORD bring us up out of Egypt?" But now the LORD has abandoned us and put us into the hand of Midian.' The LORD turned to him and said, 'Go in the strength you have and save Israel out of Midian's hand. Am I not sending you?' 'But Lord,' Gideon asked, 'how can I save Israel? My clan is the weakest in Manasseh, and I am the least in my family.'" (Judges 6:12–15) Gideon further asks for signs; first that there would be dew in the morning on a sheep skin, but the ground would be dry, then on the ground, but not on the sheep skin. God obliges and Gideon goes on to save the Israelites from the Midianites.

The Old Testament Scripture at the beginning of this sermon mentioned Jonah's second call to go to Nineveh. Let's look at the story from the beginning. *"The word of the LORD came to Jonah, son of Amittai: 'Go to the great city of Nineveh and preach against it, because its wickedness has come up before me.' But Jonah ran away from the LORD and headed for Tarshish. He went down to Joppa, where he found a ship bound for that port. After paying the fare, he went aboard and sailed for Tarshish to flee from the LORD."* Jonah 1:1–3

God called Jonah, but Jonah went fishing!

In a nutshell, God called Jonah, but rather than obey God Jonah ran (sailed) away. We're not told why Jonah ran away, but theory has it that he didn't want God to forgive the Assyrians—the people of Nineveh—a people who were bitter enemies of the Israelites!

God causes a great wind to blow across the Mediterranean Sea threatening to swamp the boat. The crew tries to save the ship, people and cargo, but they aren't getting anywhere, so they throw all the cargo into the sea to lighten the ship. Running out of options, the Captain tries to find out who is the cause of this mighty wind, believing it to be from one of the gods. After casting lots to confirm that it was Jonah who was responsible for their plight, they asked Jonah what they can do to save themselves. Jonah says, *"'Pick me up and throw me into the sea,' he replied, 'and it will become calm.*

I know that it is my fault that this great storm has come upon you (Jonah 1:12)

The ship's crew asks God to forgive them for this man's death then they throw Jonah overboard. The sea grows calm, the ship and crew are saved and they worship and praise the true God. Meanwhile, Jonah is swallowed by a "great fish." After a very interesting monolog by Jonah, the fish deposits him on land. Then Jonah gets the second call to go to Nineveh.

The most astonishing thing about the story is that Nineveh was a large city in a heathen nation (Assyria, which is modern day Iran), and yet when Jonah began preaching, the word spread like wildfire. From the lowest person to the king himself, they repented and put on sackcloth and ashes! Some scholars have said that if Jonah was in the belly of a large fish (or whale), his hair and skin would have been bleached by the stomach fluid of the fish and he must have looked quite like a ghost! So you can imagine this strange looking person coming into town saying "yet 40 days and Nineveh will be destroyed!" That must have been quite a sight.

The important point about the story is that Jonah was called to deliver a message. Jonah ran away. God told Jonah a second time to go and deliver the message (after a bit of convincing), and because Jonah finally did what God wanted him to, all the people repented. Jonah still complained to God, saying he knew God would forgive them, that's why he didn't want to go! God has the last word though. *"But Nineveh has more than a hundred and twenty thousand people who cannot tell their right hand from their left, and many cattle as well. Should I not be concerned about that great city?"* (Jonah 4:11)

In Acts chapter 10, we read about a Roman Centurion named Cornelius, who prayed, supported the local synagogue and was very devout. One day an angel appeared to him and told him to send for a man named Peter, because he (Cornelius) needed to hear what Peter had to say. Why couldn't the angel tell Cornelius what needed to be said? GOD DEPENDS ON US! For some reason, God depends on man to spread the word of salvation. Think about these 8 words: *Without God, I can't: Without ME, God won't.* Peter came to Cornelius, told the story of Jesus, and everyone in the house received

R ...oly Spirit and began praising God. Now they knew the whole ...y about salvation.

The people whom God called in the Old and New Testament were people like you and me. *"Elijah was a man just like us. He prayed earnestly that it would not rain, and it did not rain on the land for three and a half years. Again he prayed, and the heavens gave rain, and the earth produced its crops."* (James 5:17–18)

Amos was living in Judah (the southern kingdom) and God called him to go to Israel (the northern kingdom) to prophesy against the people. The King of Israel told Amos to go to his own country and earn his living as a prophet. Hear what Amos tells the king: *"...I was neither a prophet nor a prophet's son, but I was a shepherd, and I also took care of sycamore–fig trees. But the LORD took me from tending the flock and said to me, 'Go, prophesy to my people Israel.'"* (Amos 7:14–15)

It should be apparent that God decides what needs to be done and who should do it. If God calls us, He will give us the ability to do the task.

Jesus is Lord and Savior. We understand Jesus as our Savior; He died on the cross to take away our sin. But do we know Him as LORD? Have you made Jesus LORD of your life? That means allowing Him to lead you in any way that He desires. Or are you still saying (as I did for a long time), "I can't" or "I won't?"

God doesn't call everyone to proclaim His truth to the nations. God doesn't call everyone to be a preacher, teacher or miracle worker. But God does call everyone. What talent has God given you to help in the Body of Christ? When Moses was told to build the "tent of meeting" (the Tabernacle) in the desert, God said, *"See, I have chosen Bezalel son of Uri, the son of Hur, of the tribe of Judah, and I have filled him with the Spirit of God, with skill, ability and knowledge in all kinds of crafts—to make artistic designs for work in gold, silver and bronze, to cut and set stones, to work in wood, and to engage in all kinds of craftsmanship. Moreover, I have appointed Oholiab son of Ahisamach, of the tribe of Dan, to help him. Also I have given skill to all the craftsmen to make everything I have commanded you."* (Exodus 31:2–6) Whether it's a tent in the desert or a church on a hill,

God has given us all talents to work together to keep our place worship and study functioning and growing! It takes many hands to accomplish all that needs to be done.

Age does not matter (Moses was 80 when God called him, and Jeremiah was "only a child"). God has uniquely designed each of us to fit together like a puzzle. Some are leaders, some are volunteer workers, some are listeners. Yes, even listeners are needed. Listeners can lighten the burden of the shut–in and hospitalized.

How do I know if I'm being called and how do I know what God wants me to do? It's the servant's heart that God loves. Ask God to use you. Ask God to make it clear how, when, and where God wants to use you. Then be willing to go in that direction. Pray about every decision and let God lead you.

There is a line in Amazing Grace that says: "I once was lost, but now am found, was blind, but now I see." If you have been found and you see, why not help those who are still in the dark. You and I—and the church—are here for that reason. God is calling. Will you answer?

Chapter V: God is Doing a New Thing

Harley Davidson

The previous chapter was going to be the end of the book, but God has added another chapter. When I was young, I dreamed of having and riding a motorcycle. I even remember the color–green. That just didn't happen, and my parents were against riding motorcycles so I never gave a thought to owning one as I got older. I even remember a terrible accident right in front of our house and Mom and I trying to comfort the rider while we waited for the ambulance (which we had called). There was just no way I could even consider riding a motorcycle.

When God arranges things though, should we turn the other way and ignore the direction God has prepared for us? While living near Laurel, Maryland, I noticed a building being constructed near the Baltimore Washington Parkway and I naturally wondered what sort of business it would be. I first thought it was going to be a restaurant, especially when the "Old Glory" sign went up. "Glory Days" was a restaurant in Bowie, and this building looked like a restaurant, so that must be it. Then one day another sign was placed near the building. On a tall pole was a large sign that you really couldn't miss, and this took away all doubt about the building's purpose. The sign said "Harley Davidson." Now I really couldn't wait for it to open. I grew up near York, Pennsylvania, and that's where some models of Harley Davidson motorcycles were made. The factory offered tours, but I had never taken the tour or gone to even see the motorcycles. Like most people, I had only seen a motorcycle by chance, here and there. I was anxious to go look at them up close.

Finally a banner was posted announced the date for an openi. celebration. Actually, there were two "soft" openings and then the grand opening. I attended the grand opening and noticed four tents set up in the parking lot. Three of those tents were for witnessing by Christian motorcycle groups! I was excited. Could I ride a motorcycle with Christians? Somehow I hadn't necessarily associated Christians with motorcycles. I was about to be educated in a very good way!

As soon as I discovered this dealership offered a licensing rider's class, I put my name on the list. When I was told that the riding part of the class was on Saturday and Sunday mornings, I asked if they would do the riding at any other time since I went to church on Sunday morning. They informed me that a class would be held at another time but it wasn't finalized yet. But, it wasn't going to happen, at least not now.

Soon after Old Glory opened, we moved and I discovered another Harley Davidson dealer just as close to us at our new location. Although this dealership did not have a riding course available, they directed me to a local college where the course was offered.

Now for the REAL God–incidents! Normally the riding part of the course is on Saturday morning and Sunday morning, even for the college course. I had already said I would not miss church on Sunday morning (and I thought, "If God wants me to do this, He will provide a way"). Well, it just happened (HA! There is no such thing as "co–incidents", only "God–incidents!") that they were offering a class with riding on Saturday afternoon and Sunday afternoon. Not only that, but the class had been cancelled and then reestablished, so it was not full. All other classes were full for the year.

Yet another surprise awaited me when I signed up for the class. I asked the registrar if I received any discount for being a senior citizen, and the young lady said, "I already took care of it." Old Glory in Laurel, Maryland, charged $330 for the riding course. The college charged $297. With my senior citizen discount I ended up paying just $97. Thank you Lord! Also, there were only 4 people in our class, so we received almost one–on–one training as there were two instructors. It was amazing. After the required class time (weekday evenings) at the college, we headed out to the practice and area a mile or so from the school for the riding practice and Saturday afternoon and Sunday afternoon we rode through obstacles and at the end of the Sunday riding, we were graded on the proficiency of our ride through the obstacles. The interesting thing is that I got my license (certificate) on my 62nd birthday. God's timing is always perfect. What a birthday gift!

So what does this have to do with God? (Other than the "God–incidents") Well, I met many Christian riders during the following three years and many who need to know Jesus. I became a Chaplain for the local chapter of a national organization and have held Bible studies for the chapter members. During each chapter meeting I lift up prayers for members' concerns. On one two–day ride, we even had a worship service presented by another rider and me. Riding a motorcycle would never have entered my mind if it had not been for the circumstances leading up to this day. I firmly believe God directed every part of it. God brought me to this Christian motorcycle group for a reason, and my desire is to build up the faith of the members so that everyone will be equipped to reach out to the biker community in the name of Jesus.

Our local chapter is made up of people from differe denominational churches as well as non–denominational churches. Another goal is to "lower the walls" and work (and act) as Christians, not denominations. So far we have done this pretty well, but there is more to learn. Studying the Bible goes a long way to get us back to a common goal. We are all to be sharing the Gospel with those who need to hear it.

As I mentioned, prayers are lifted up during the chapter meetings, and at our last meeting we actually had more praise reports than prayer concerns! Now that's God at work! Prayers are being answered in awesome ways!

Hardly a week goes by that I haven't prayed for someone or invited them to come to our chapter meetings. Of course it's all about Jesus, but just like church, if you get their interest, you get to tell them the whole story. Besides, I have a vest with a Christian message. They know Who I really represent.

Never Ending Story

All stories have to have an ending, but God's story never ends. I will continue to preach, pray, teach and write as long as I am able. Perhaps God will continually show me His awesome power and love so that I can bless others. Some believe by hearing the Word. Some require miracles to believe. I believe God gets our attention by the method He knows will be most effective. It is my fervent hope that this book will bless many by revealing God working in–and through–one ordinary life.

Matthew 9:37-38 *"Then He said to His disciples, 'The harvest truly is plentiful, but the laborers are few. Therefore pray the Lord of the harvest to send out laborers into His harvest.'"*

The End